LORCA

SELECTED POEMS

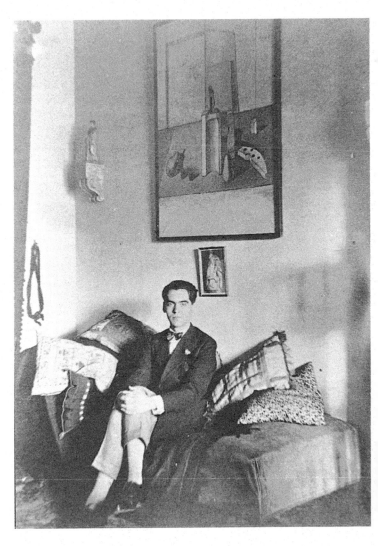

Lorca in his house in Granada, 1925, below Salvador Dalí's
oil painting 'Soda siphon and Bottle of Rum'

FEDERICO GARCÍA

Lorca

Selected Poems

INTRODUCED AND EDITED BY

J. L. Gili

WITH PLAIN
PROSE TRANSLATIONS
OF EACH POEM

Anvil Press Poetry

This edition published in 2010
by Anvil Press Poetry Ltd
Neptune House 70 Royal Hill London SE10 8RF
www.anvilpresspoetry.com
First published by Penguin Books in 1960
This edition copyright © Herederos de Federico García Lorca 2010

ISBN 978 0 85646 388 4

This book is published
with financial assistance from Arts Council England

A catalogue record for this book
is available from the British Library

Designed and set in Monotype Bembo by Anvil

PREFACE

THIS book was first published in the old Penguin Poets series of foreign texts with 'plain prose' translations, whose general editor was J. M. Cohen, himself a distinguished scholar and translator. The series was intended to 'make a fair selection of the world's finest poetry available to readers who could not, but for the translations at the foot of each page, approach it without dictionaries and a slow plodding from line to line.' These editions, he wrote, were 'not intended only for those with a command of languages. They should appeal also to the adventurous who, for sheer love of poetry, will attack a poem in a tongue almost unknown to them, guided only by their previous reading and some Latin or French.'

Joan Gili's deep knowledge and love of Spanish poetry and Lorca's work shine through his introduction and the sensitive yet unassuming renderings of his chosen poems and telling extracts from the plays. His addition of Lorca's lecture on the *duende* is an inspired bonus; it is one of the great essays on the spirit of poetry.

For many of my generation their first encounter with Lorca was through this book and a better introduction is hard to imagine. Many translations of Lorca's poems must owe their existence to it. For example, Ted Hughes said in his *Paris Review* interview (1995) that he had discovered the work of Lorca through this book. An interesting article by the Spanish poet and translator Jordi Doce ('The Marriage of Words', Centre for Ted Hughes Studies, April 2004) traces the roots of Hughes' version of *Blood Wedding*, premiered in London in 1996, back to his reading of the Penguin book and demonstrates that *Blood Wedding* and Gili's version of Lorca's essay on the *duende* 'were united early on in his imagination'.

The book was retired by its first publisher after many years in print and was replaced in 1997 by Christopher Maurer's excellent bilingual *Selected Poems* with verse translations. But

Gili's is a different kind of book and still has its place. We are more than glad to bring it back, with the benefit of the added Spanish text of the *duende* lecture, a number of corrections suggested by Christopher Maurer (see the Note on the Text, p. 188) as well as a handful of alterations to his translations which Gili had made. Among them perhaps most notable is the repeated line in 'Somnambular Ballad', over the translation of which much argument has taken place – almost every time, in fact, that the poem is discussed: 'Verde que te quiero verde.' In the old edition this read: 'Green, green, I love you green.' It is now the plainer and more forceful 'Green, I want you green.'

THE PUBLISHER

CONTENTS

PREFACE   5
INTRODUCTION   11

from Libro de poemas (1921)

    Balada de la placeta   27
    Balada de un día de Julio   30
    La balada del agua del mar   34
    Sueño   36
    Cantos nuevos   37
    Deseo   38

from Poema del cante jondo (1921)

    Baladilla de los tres ríos   40
    Paisaje   41
    La guitarra   42
    Pueblo   43
    Paso   44
    Camino   45
    La Lola   46
    Malagueña   47

from Canciónes (1921–4)

    Canción de jinete (1860)   48
    Canción de jinete   48
    Es verdad   50
    Canción   51
    La luna asoma   52
    Serenata   53
    El niño mudo   54
    Despedida   54
    Suicidio   55
    Granada y 1850   56
    Canción del naranjo seco   57

from Mariana Pineda (1925)

Romance de la talabartera 58

from Romancero gitano (1924–7)

Romance de la luna, luna 61
Reyerta 63
Romance sonámbulo 65
La monja gitana 69
La casada infiel 71
Romance de la pena negra 73
San Gabriel (Sevilla) 75
Prendimiento de Antoñito el Camborio 78
Muerte de Antoñito el Camborio 81
Romance del emplazado 83
Romance le la Guardia Civil española 86
Thamar y Amnón 92

from Poeta en Nueva York (1929–30)

El rey de Harlem 96
La aurora 103
Poema doble del lago Eden 104
Cielo vivo 107
Oda a Walt Whitman 109
Pequeño poema infinito 116

from Bodas de sangre (1933)

Nana 118
Monólogo de la luna 122
«Era hermoso jinete» 124

from Yerma (1935)

«¿De dónde vienes, amor, mi niño?» 127
«¿Por qué duermes solo, pastor?» 128
«¡Ay, qué prado de pena!» 129

Llanto por Ignacio Sánchez Mejías (1935)

La cogida y la muerte   130
La sangre derramada   133
Cuerpo presente   137
Alma ausente   140

from Diván del Tamarit (1936)

Gacela de la terrible presencia   142
Gacela de la muerte oscura   143
Gacela de la huida   145
Casida del herido por el agua   146
Casida del llanto   147
Casida de los ramos   148
Casida de la mujer tendida   149
Casida de la rosa   150
Casida de las palomas oscuras   151

Miscellaneous Poems

Cada canción   152
Canto nocturno de los marineros andaluces   153
Norma   155
Adán   156

Juego y teoría del duende   158
Theory and Function of the *Duende*   159

NOTE ON THE TEXT   188
INDEX OF FIRST LINES   189
INDEX OF TITLES   191

INTRODUCTION

No OTHER contemporary Spanish poet has achieved so international a reputation as Lorca. Already, in the years preceding the Second World War, translations of his work had made him well known, especially in Britain and the Americas. In part, perhaps, his early fame outside Spain may be attributable to the tragic and violent circumstances of his death in the Spanish Civil War. But succeeding years have proved that the major part of his popularity rests on surer foundations than mere sensationalism. Indeed, the figure of Lorca has gained in perspective with the years, and it may now be asserted with confidence that his poetry is among the best which Spain has produced. The present selection (with his essay on the *Duende* as an appendix) contains the essential in Lorca's poetry.

Federico García Lorca was born at Fuentevaqueros, in the fertile plain of Granada, on 5 June 1898. He was murdered in August 1936 by a group of unknown persons during the first days of the Civil War. The assassination took place, it seems, at Viznar, on the hills outside Granada, but his body (as he prophetically foresaw) has never been found:

> . . . *comprendí que me habían asesinado.*
> *Recorrieron los cafés y los cementerios y las iglesias,*
> *abrieron los toneles y los armarios,*
> *destrozaron tres esqueletos para arrancar sus dientes de oro.*
> *Ya no me encontraron.*
> *¿No me encontraron?*
> *No. No me encontraron★*

★ . . . I realised I had been murdered. They searched cafés and cemeteries and churches, they opened barrels and cupboards, they plundered three skeletons to remove their gold teeth. They did not find me. They never found me? No. They never found me.

'My father was a farmer, a rich man, and a good horseman,' he once said to an interviewer, 'and my mother came from a distinguished family.' He was the eldest of a family of two brothers and two sisters. The first years of his life were spent on the family farm. Owing to a serious illness soon after his birth, he was unable to walk until he was four. He was left with a slight limp hardly noticeable when he was grown-up. But, as his friend R. M. Nadal has pointed out, this physical handicap considerably influenced the formation of his character (without, however, spoiling his natural gaiety). Inability to join in other children's games increased his powers of imagination and perception, and he expressed himself in make-believe – theatres, marionettes, processions, and dressing-up the old family servants and his younger brothers, thus drawing the family circle round him. With his first savings he bought a toy-theatre in Granada. The fact that there were no printed plays included in the purchase did not deter young Federico, who proceeded to write his own. From then on he never lost his interest in the theatre, which was to become an integral part of his work.

There were no spectacular intellectual achievements in his early years. His mother – once a teacher – taught him his first letters. Life was peaceful and happy on the family farm; there he lived in close contact with the countryside and the life of the village, rich in Andalusian tradition. He could hum popular airs even before he learned to speak, and from the old servants he learned folk-tales and popular *romances* or ballads. Much of what he was absorbing now would later be assimilated into his poetry. It was, as he later acknowledged, an initiation into poetic experience. The following cradle song, of which he was very fond:

> *A la nana, nana, nana,*
> *a la nanito de aquel*

> *que llevó el caballo al agua*
> *y lo dejó sin beber...* ★

and from which he drew inspiration for his lullaby in *Bodas de Sangre*, is an example of the simple lyric incantation on which he was nourished.

When the time came for Federico's schooling to be taken seriously in hand, the family moved to Granada. There he enjoyed the usual education of a boy in his social position until he reached University age. He started his University studies at Granada University, but never finished them – in the same way in which he never finished his studies when he went to Madrid. He was never in the least academically inclined: his interests lay outside the University curriculum. He was happier in the cafés, talking to friends; exploring the countryside or the gardens of Granada; discovering the many cultures and traditions that went to make the ancient country of Andalusia; and getting to know the gipsies, who were destined to be one of the major inspirations of his work. He learned to play the piano and the guitar, although he soon abandoned the latter. He met Manuel de Falla, who became a great friend and master, and who encouraged and guided him in the collecting of traditional folk-songs and in setting them to music.

The greater part of his reading was done outside his set books: it included the classics, in translation, especially Greek plays, Shakespeare, Ibsen, Victor Hugo, Maeterlinck, the Spanish classics, the works of those writers belonging to the so-called '98 generation, such as Machado, Unamuno, Azorín; also the Spanish Romantic poets and contemporary poets, from Rubén Darío to Juan Ramón Jiménez.

★ Impossible to translate, but the following is an approximation:
'Hushaby, hushaby, hushaby, the little lullaby of the one who led his horse to the water and did not let him drink...'

His friends in Granada were painters, sculptors, musicians, and poets. With de Falla he organized a festival of *cante jondo*, the 'deep song' of Southern Spain, and it was then that he came into closer contact with the gipsy world; its singers and dancers. J. B. Trend wrote that many 'cultured' people in Spain became at that time interested in the *cante jondo* 'because they wished to acquire something of the oldest culture in the Peninsula'. No doubt Lorca was drawn to this society for the same reasons.

While still in Granada, Lorca published his first prose book, *Impresiones y paisajes* (1918), the result of many trips around Spain with a group headed by his Professor of Art at the University of Granada. This series of narratives already shows the poet's personality, and marks the end of his youthful period.

In the following year he went to Madrid, ostensibly with the purpose of continuing his studies. There, as in Granada, his interests were again in the main non-academic. It was his good fortune, however, that he was advised for his studies to enter the *Residencia de Estudiantes*, an institution of great liberal tradition. The *Residencia* also sheltered many poets of note: Antonio Machado, Juan Ramón Jiménez, J. Moreno Villa, Pedro Salinas, Rafael Alberti, Jorge Guillén. In the President of the *Residencia*, Don Alberto Jiménez, he found a friend who was aware of Lorca's worth and gave him every facility which would enable him to develop his personality. There he produced plays, composed at the piano,* painted (or drew with crayons), transcribed folk-songs, and recited his poems – a favourite occupation. In this congenial atmosphere he came also into contact with other Spanish intellectuals of note – Unamuno and Ortega y Gasset were often

---

* He is not in fact known to have composed music while living at the *Residencia*: his only known piano compositions are from years earlier, and the arrangements of folksongs, done for La Argentinita, are later. [Ed.]

to be found there – and several leading international writers who gave lectures at the *Residencia*, such as Bergson, Valéry, Claudel, Aragon, Chesterton, Keynes, H. G. Wells, etc. He stayed there for many years, never finishing his studies, but constantly working and perfecting his poetry, and fully conscious now of his calling as a poet.

Futurism, Dadaism, and other revolutionary developments in the European post-war literary scenes were exerting their influence on several of Lorca's contemporaries in Madrid; but he himself, by nature unsympathetic to cliques, seems at first to have been only remotely affected. In fact, it was not until his friendship with Salvador Dalí, the outstanding exponent of Surrealism, who lived in the *Residencia* for a time, that he showed any vital awareness of contemporary currents. But whether contemporary or traditional, any influence he received was quickly assimilated into his own poetical idiom, often unconsciously. A word or a phrase heard would one day appear in a poem, without his being aware of it. It was all part of his spontaneous approach to his art. Guillermo de Torre, speaking of Lorca's assimilation and subsequent recreation of Andalusian folk-songs, says: 'He sings them, he dreams them, he discovers them again – in a word, he turns them into poetry.' In this same connexion, his brother Francisco says: 'During an excursion to the Sierra Nevada, the mule driver who was leading sang to himself:

> *Y yo que me la llevé al río*
> *creyendo que era mozuela,*
> *pero tenía marido.* ★

Sometime later, one day when we were speaking of the ballad "The Faithless Wife", I reminded Federico of the mule driver's song. To my enormous surprise, he had completely

---

★ And I took her to the river believing her a maid, but she had a husband.

forgotten it. He thought the first three lines of the ballad were as much his as the rest of the poem. More than that, I thought I could tell that he did not like my insistence for he continued to believe that I was mistaken.'

His first book of poems, *Libro de poemas*, was published in 1921 without attracting much attention outside his circle; but in any case he was essentially averse to committing himself to print. His literary friends had to use countless stratagems in order to extract a poem from him for one of their periodicals. Although he wrote many poems after 1921, his next book of poems, *Canciones*, did not appear until 1927. Such was the strength of his personality, how ever, that before his important work appeared his influence on other poets was already noticeable. He preferred reading his poems, because as he said in his revealing essay on the *duende*, poetry requires as interpreter a living body. It was by these readings, more than by his printed work, that he exercised his influence. It was Roy Campbell who pointed out this while comparing him to Dylan Thomas, who also extracted the maximum of meaning from words through their sound, probably because they both were born in countries where the musical and vocal tradition is very strong among the people.

In order to understand the *duende*, the magic, of his personality it is worth quoting what his contemporaries have said. The poet Rafael Alberti wrote: 'A discharge as of electric sympathy, a spell, an irresistible atmosphere of magic which surrounded and imprisoned his audience, flowed from him while he talked, recited, improvised a scene from a play, or sang, accompanying himself at the piano. Because everywhere Lorca went he found a piano.' Even the poet Pedro Salinas, his senior by seven years, said: 'He was the feast, the gaiety that started up before us, and we had no alternative but to follow him.' This gay, irresistible personality was in part due to his histrionic temperament, which did

not exclude his darker moods. His close friend the poet Vicente Aleixandre tells how he had seen him 'in the loftiness of the night suddenly look out from some mysterious balustrades, when the moonlight shone full on his face; and I have felt his arms resting on the air, but his feet sinking into Time, into centuries, into the most remote root of the Spanish soil'. This duality in his character reflects the character of Spain itself; at once gay and darkly sombre.

Apart from an early play, *El maleficio de la mariposa* (The Butterfly's Evil Spell), performed in Madrid in 1920, his first theatrical venture to prove successful was the historical drama in verse *Mariana Pineda*, performed in Madrid in 1927. It is interesting to see how his development as a dramatist ran parallel to his development as a poet. He would have agreed with T. S. Eliot when he says 'the ideal medium for poetry, and the most direct means of social 'usefulness' for poetry, is the theatre'. For Lorca was socially conscious: he believed that the poet in 'this dramatic moment of the world, has to laugh and cry with the people'.

The following year saw the publication of his most popular book, the *Romancero gitano*, which became an immediate success in Spain and in all Spanish-speaking countries. The book consists of ballads, mostly on gipsy themes, written in the traditional *romance* form, with an assonance in every second line. Their apparent facility belies the poet's consummate technical skill. All the ingredients characterizing his poetry are there: his evocative feeling, his sensuousness, the whole gipsy mythology, his awareness of death, his brilliant but never superfluous metaphors. As with all Lorca's poetry, it would not be difficult to find precedents for much of this work. The first lines of the famous 'Romance sonámbulo' are more than reminiscent of Juan Ramón Jiménez's poem beginning 'Verde es la niña. Tiene verdes ojos, pelo verde.' But the similarity goes no farther, in the same way as the muleteer's song was the starting point for the ballad of

'La casada infiel'. And precedents could even be found farther back in the 'verdes voces' of Góngora,* for example, or in popular balladry; but all this would only confirm the fact that Lorca was steeped in Spanish tradition, a tradition ending for him in Juan Ramón Jiménez.

In the *Romancero gitano* Lorca reaches the perfect fusion of the popular with the artistic, the traditional with the modern. Perhaps in this lies the universal appeal of much of his work, for there is no break in Lorca between the modern and the traditional; rather, the traditional is kept alive by the very newness of his approach to poetry.

Lorca was not writing for a minority as were most poets of his generation. He wanted the 'images I build of my characters to be understood by the characters themselves'. It was inherent in his nature that he should need to be understood, to be loved through his poetry by everyone. That he succeeded nobody doubts, for even quite illiterate people understand, or if they do not quite understand, at least they sense what the poet says. Arturo Barea, in his *Lorca, the Poet and the People*, dwells on this point and gives instances of the reaction of simple labourers on hearing Lorca's poetry. His is a poetry in which the sensuous sound of the words evokes visual impressions, and this is what gives the gipsy ballads a dramatic and emotional appeal. We feel strongly the impact of the fundamental passions woven through the narrative, of love, sorrow, and death – the central theme in most of the ballads, and one of the major obsessions in Lorca's work. In poetry, he said, 'the *duende* does not come unless he sees the possibility of death'. And Spain, being always moved by the *duende*, is necessarily a 'nation of death, a nation open to death . . . a dead person in Spain is more alive when dead than is the case anywhere else . . . a country where what matters most has the ultimate quality of death'. From the

---

* It was Lorca, not Góngora. who spoke of *verdes voces* (green voices). [Ed.]

earliest Spanish lyrics onwards this is basically true. Lorca's greatest poem was inspired, as we shall see, by the death of his friend the bullfighter Ignacio Sánchez Mejías.

It may at first seem perplexing that the great popularity which the *Romancero gitano* brought Lorca should have weighed heavily on him. Such was his dislike of labels, however, that he did not wish to be acclaimed the poet of the gipsies. He did not want to become a victim of his own success. 'The gipsies,' he said, 'are a theme, and nothing else. I could just as well be the poet of sewing needles or hydro-electric landscapes.' He went through a period of deep depression. 'Now I am writing a poetry which demands the opening of veins, a poetry freed from reality,' he wrote to a friend. The way for *Poeta en Nueva York* was now open.

When the opportunity came for a trip to the USA, he did not hesitate. He arrived at New York in the summer of 1929, and through his *Residencia* contacts he was admitted to Columbia University, and joined a course of English for foreigners, from which he withdrew after the first week as he felt himself incapable of learning the language. He stayed at Columbia University, however, until the spring of the following year, with brief journeys to the Vermont countryside.

He began writing the poems which were later gathered under the title of *Poeta en Nueva York*, published posthumously in 1940. He had no illusions as to what he would find in America:

> Yo he venido para ver la turbia sangre.
> La sangre que lleva las máquinas a las cataratas
> y el espíritu a la lengua de la cobra.★

For him New York was a town of 'extra-human architecture

★ I have come to see the turbid blood. The blood that takes the machines to the cataracts, and our soul to the cobra's tongue.

and of furious rhythm, geometry, and anguish'. A world so alien to his sun-drenched Andalusia created a conflict in his poetic world. It could not be expected that Lorca would speak now with the same voice as in the *Canciones* or the *Romancero gitano*. He would need a different technique to express the complexities of his emotions, and in surrealist imagery he found the medium that fitted his present mood. Before he left Madrid there had already been some experiments in this direction, such as the 'Oda al Santísimo Sacramento del Altar' and the 'Oda a Salvador Dalí', and some prose sketches of a surrealist nature, doubtless the result of his close association with Salvador Dalí and other Catalan and Spanish surrealist artists. There were also, preceding *Poeta en Nueva York*, his abstract drawings, his public defence of Joan Miró and Dalí's work, and the part he played in a proposed surrealist manifesto. These precedents are often forgotten by those who take this book as a solitary example, and unrepresentative of Lorca's work. This may explain why *Poeta en Nueva York* is the least understood of his works, especially in the Spanish-speaking world. In fact, most of Lorca's basic ingredients are to be found here, but in the context of surrealist imagery, and in the drama of the Negroes and of the white-man imprisoned in a world of machinery, which he has substituted for the drama of the gipsies. His warmth of feeling for the Negro was very real:

> *No hay angustia comparable a tus rojos oprimidos,*
> *a tu sangre estremecida dentro del eclipse oscuro,*
> *a tu violencia granate sordomuda en la penumbra.**

If *Poeta en Nueva York* is surrealist, it is surrealism after his own peculiar manner. His writing has a tension which is not

---

* There is no anguish to compare with your oppressed reds, or with the shudder of your blood within the dark eclipse, or with your garnet-coloured violence deaf and dumb in the half-light.

found in the work of other surrealists, a passionate attachment to solid reality just as much as to the visionary images that arise from it. In the same way in which he used earlier traditional Spanish forms for his own ends, he now uses surrealism, which in some of the poems suggests in its style an affinity with Walt Whitman, whom he read in translation while in New York. The American Conrad Aiken saw this very dearly when he wrote: 'Lorca devoured all the properties of surrealism, stuffed his cheeks with them, like a conjurer, blew them out of his mouth again as poems – but so he did with everything else he fed on.' In spite of its apparent singularity, then, *Poeta en Nueva York* fits into the main stream of Lorca's work. It is a book of great poetic value, dramatic, complex, and completely actual.

By the spring of 1930 the poet felt the need for brighter landscapes, and when he received an invitation to lecture in Havana he accepted it with alacrity and set forth for that 'beautiful island of the burning sun'. He stayed in Cuba about two months, happy in the Latin atmosphere of the island. In the melodious rhythms of Cuban songs he discovered the Spanish tradition he knew so well, and perhaps this led him to a change of mood, back to the original source of his inspiration, with roots more firmly secure in the Andalusian, the Spanish, and the religious, which together form the basis of his work. The two main lectures he delivered in Cuba* affirm his reinstatement of basic Spanish principles of tradition: one on children's songs, or cradle-songs, and the other on the *duende*, not the ghostly spirit as the exact translation of the word signifies, but the creative vivifying spirit known to every Andalusian artist.

---

* The lecture on *duende* was given not in 1930 in Havana (where he spoke on 'Imagination, Inspiration and Evasion') but three years later, in Buenos Aires and Montevideo. [Ed.]

On his return to Spain, he stayed for a while in his father's country house near Granada. Now the most fruitful period of his life began. Before the end of 1930 his poetical play *La zapatera prodigiosa* (The Shoemaker's Prodigious Wife), which he had begun while in New York, was staged in Madrid. Some of his New York poems began to appear in various periodicals, notably in the *Revista de Occidente* of which J. Ortega y Gasset was the editor.

In the following year a new book of poems, *Poema del cante jondo*, was published. It is a book belonging to the earlier period of *Canciones*, and deriving from the days when the author, together with de Falla, organized the festival of *cante jondo*. What Lorca said on the occasion of the festival could equally be applied to this work: 'By revealing its ancient song, we are trying to discover the soul of Andalusia.' The poet used here Andalusian folk-lore elements which he had unconsciously absorbed in his early years, together with others consciously derived from his researches into popular poetry. He was a firm believer in the value of the anonymous village poet, who 'extracts in three or four lines all the rare complexity of the highest sentimental moments in the life of man. There are *coplas* in which the lyrical emotion reaches a point only attained by a few rare poets.

> *Cerco tiene la luna*
> *mi amor ha muerto.* ★

In these two popular lines there is more mystery than in the dramas of Maeterlinck, a simple, real, clean mystery . . .'

With the advent of the Republic in 1931, he saw the opportunity of bringing the theatre to the people, and submitted to the Government a scheme for a travelling theatre, with university students as actors. This resulted in the company *La Barraca*, which, following the tradition of strolling

---

★ The moon is fenced in, my love has died.

players, travelled (with Lorca as general producer and director) to remote Spanish villages, where it performed plays by Lope de Vega, Calderón, and other Spanish classics, often with incidental music arranged by the poet. These peasant audiences, attending the performances with appreciative reverence, were seeing a play for the first time, and their simple reactions provided Lorca with an invaluable experience for the plays he was yet to write.

The first of his poetical tragedies, *Bodas de sangre* (Blood Wedding), was performed in Madrid in 1933. It was an immediate success, and the success was repeated when he took the play to Buenos Aires, where he stayed until the following spring, helping in the production of the play, giving some lectures, and producing successfully a play by Lope de Vega.

On his return to Madrid, *Yerma*, the second tragedy, was presented on the Madrid stage in 1934. It is a play, like the previous one, of Andalusian peasant life, with frustrated maternity as its theme. He completed the trilogy with *La casa de Bernarda Alba* (The House of Bernarda Alba), which was published and performed posthumously, a play of grim realism written for the most part in prose. In this play five daughters in love with the same man are repressed by a domineering mother.

Lorca's plays spring from the same source as his poetry, and to them he devoted a great part of his life. He believed that the theatre was poetry made human, and it was because of his need for human contact that he was so much attracted to the theatre. It provided him also with the means to express himself in a tragic form, inherent in his poetry. But it was not only tragedy that occupied his attention now, for after *Yerma* he was writing an evocative and romantic play in an end-of-the-nineteenth-century setting, a play of *bourgeois* life in Granada, *Doña Rosita la soltera, o el lenguaje de las flores* (Doña Rosita, the Spinster, or The Language of Flowers),

performed in Barcelona in 1935, a play of 'sweet ironies' as he put it. There were also other plays such as *Así que pasen cinco años* (As Soon as Five Years Pass), published after his death, which is an almost surrealist *divertissement*.

During these fertile years he did not abandon the writing of pure poetry. A new book of poems was in preparation, the *Diván del Tamarit*. Then suddenly he was stunned by the death of his close friend the bullfighter Ignacio Sánchez Mejías, and wrote almost without a stop his great elegy in four movements, the *Llanto por Ignacio Sánchez Mejías* (Lament for Ignacio Sánchez Mejías), one of the finest poems in contemporary Spanish literature. He used for each section or movement a different metre, thereby enhancing the dramatic effect of the work as a whole. Death triumphs at last,

> *¡Y el toro solo corazón arriba!*★

In this, the most mature and poignant of his poems, we find crystallized all the richness of his poetic mind. What he said of his friend is indeed true of himself:

> *Tardará mucho tiempo en nacer, si es que nace,*
> *un andaluz tan claro, tan rico de aventura.*†

While finishing the last tragedy in his trilogy, *La casa de Bernarda Alba*, he was also engaged in a book of sonnets, *Sonetos del amor oscuro*.‡ The manuscript of these sonnets was lost, it seems irrevocably, during the Civil War. The extent of the loss may be judged by the following words of the poet Vicente Aleixandre: 'He was reading me his *Sonetos*

★ And the bull alone exultant!

† Not for a long time will be born, if ever, an Andalusian so noble, so rich in adventure.

‡ Rough drafts of the extant 'Sonetos del amor oscuro' were published in pirated and authorized editions in 1983–84. [Ed.]

del amor oscuro, a prodigy of passion, of enthusiasm, of happiness, of torment, pure and ardent monument to love in which the prime material is now the poet's flesh, his heart, his soul wide open to his own destruction. Wonder-struck, I gazed at him and said: "Federico, what a heart! How much you must have loved, how much you must have suffered!"'

The poet's life, at the height of his artistic development, was cut short by the ignoble murder. His work and his personality were inseparable, and his own tribute to the poet Góngora might well be applied to himself: 'A Góngora no hay que leerlo, hay que amarlo.'★

For the Spanish text I have followed, but for one or two exceptions, the edition of *Obras Completas* (Madrid, 1957). The poems are arranged chronologically. I am indebted to the General Editor of the series, J. M. Cohen, for his valuable and constructive suggestions. I wish also to express my gratitude to my wife, Elizabeth, for her patient help at every stage of the work, and to C. Henry Warren for his painstaking reading of the manuscript. My debt to Stephen Spender dates back to some of the translations we published in collaboration twenty years ago, and although the present translation is entirely new and the selection very much enlarged, I have benefited from our previous work. His beautiful rendering into sonnet form of my plain translation of 'Adán', I have left exactly as he wrote it.

J. L. G.

Oxford, April 1959

★ Góngora does not have to be read – he has to be loved.

BALADA DE LA PLACETA

CANTAN los niños
en la noche quieta:
¡Arroyo claro,
fuente serena!

LOS NIÑOS

¿Qué tiene tu divino
corazón en fiesta?

YO

Un doblar de campanas,
perdidas en la niebla.

LOS NIÑOS

Ya nos dejas cantando
en la plazuela.
¡Arroyo claro,
fuente serena!

¿Qué tienes en tus manos
de primavera?

YO

Una rosa de sangre
y una azucena.

Ballad of the Little Square

THE children sing in the quiet night: Clear stream, serene fountain!
THE CHILDREN: What does your divine rejoicing heart hold?
MYSELF: A ringing of bells lost in the mist.
THE CHILDREN: You leave us singing in the little square. Clear
stream, serene fountain! What do you hold in your vernal hands?
MYSELF: A rose of blood and a white lily.

LOS NIÑOS

Mójalas en el agua
de la caución añeja.
¡Arroyo claro,
fuente serena!

¿Qué sientes en tu boca
roja y sedienta?

YO

El sabor de los huesos
de mi gran calavera.

LOS NIÑOS

Bebe el agua tranquila
de la canción añeja:
¡Arroyo claro,
fuente serena!

¿Por qué te vas tan lejos
de la plazuela?

YO

¡Voy en busca de magos
y de princesas!

THE CHILDREN: Dip them in the water of the ancient song. Clear
stream, serene fountain! What do you feel in your mouth scarlet and
thirsting?

MYSELF: The taste of the bones of my big skull!

THE CHILDREN: Drink the tranquil water of the ancient song.
Clear stream, serene fountain! Why do you go so far from the little
square?

MYSELF: I go in search of magicians and princesses!

LOS NIÑOS

¿Quién te enseñó el camino
de los poetas?

YO

La fuente y el arroyo
de la canción añeja.

LOS NIÑOS

¿Te vas lejos, muy lejos
del mar y de la tierra?

YO

Se ha llenado de luces
mi corazón de seda,
de campanas perdidas,
de lirios y de abejas,
y yo me iré muy lejos,
más allá de esas sierras,
más allá de los mares,
cerca de las estrellas,
para pedirle a Cristo
Señor que me devuelva
mi alma antigua de niño,
madura de leyendas,

THE CHILDREN: Who showed you the path of the poets?

MYSELF: The fountain and the stream of the ancient song.

THE CHILDREN: Do you go far, very far, from the sea and the earth?

MYSELF: My heart of silk is filled with lights, with lost bells, with lilies, and with bees, and I will go very far, farther than those hills, farther than the seas, close to the stars, to ask Christ the Lord to give me back my ancient soul of a child, mellowed with legends, with the

con el gorro de plumas
y el sable de madera.

Ya nos dejas cantando
en la plazuela.
¡Arroyo claro,
fuente serena!

Las pupilas enormes
de las frondas resecas,
heridas por el viento,
lloran las hojas muertas.

BALADA DE UN DÍA DE JULIO

ESQUILONES de plata
llevan los bueyes.

«¿Dónde vas, niña mía,
de sol y nieve?»

«Voy a las margaritas
del prado verde.»

feathered cap, and the wooden sword.

THE CHILDREN: You leave us singing in the little square, clear stream, serene fountain!

Enormous pupils of parched fronds, wounded by the wind, weep dead leaves.

Ballad of a Day in July

THE oxen wear large silver bells.

'Where do you go, sweet maid, of sun and snow?'

'I go to the daisies in the green meadow.'

«El prado está muy lejos
y miedo tiene.»

«Al airón y a la sombra
mi amor no teme.»

«Teme al sol, niña mía,
de sol y nieve.»

«Se fué de mis cabellos
ya para siempre.»

«¿Quién eres, blanca niña?
¿De dónde vienes?»

«Vengo de los amores
y de las fuentes.»

Esquilones de plata
llevan los bueyes.

«¿Qué llevas en la boca
que se te enciende?»

«La estrella de mi amante
que vive y muere.»

'The meadow is far away and full of fear.'
'My love does not fear the heron or the shadow.'
'Fear the sun, sweet maid, of sun and snow.'
'It has now gone from my tresses for ever.'
'Who are you, white maid? From where do you come?'
'From amours and from fountains I come.'
The oxen wear large silver bells.
'What does your mouth hold which turns to a blaze?'
'The star of my lover, living and dying.'

«¿Qué llevas en el pecho
tan fino y leve?»

«La espada de mi amante
que vive y muere.»

«¿Qué llevas en los ojos,
negro y solemne?»

«Mi pensamiento triste
que siempre hiere.»

«¿Por qué llevas un manto
negro de muerte?»

«¡Ay, yo soy la viudita,
triste y sin bienes,
del conde del Laurel
de los Laureles!»

«¿A quién buscas aquí,
si a nadie quieres?»
«Busco el cuerpo del conde
de los Laureles.»

'What does your breast hold, so sharp and slight?'
'The sword of my lover, living and dying.'
'What do your eyes hold, so black and solemn?'
'My sad remembrance for ever hurting.'
'Why do you wear a black cloak of death?'
'Alas, I am the poor widow, in want and misery, of the Count of
Laurel of the Laurels!'
'Whom do you seek here, if you love no one?'
'I seek the body of the Count of the Laurels.'

«¿Tú buscas el amor,
viudita aleve?
Tú buscas un amor
que ojalá encuentres.»

«Estrellitas del cielo
son mis quereres,
¿dónde hallaré a mi amante
que vive y muere?»

«Está muerto en el agua,
niña de nieve,
cubierto de nostalgias
y de claveles.»

«¡Ay!, caballero errante
de los cipreses,
una noche de luna
mi alma te ofrece.»

«¡Ah Isis soñadora!
Niña sin mieles,
la que en boca de niños
su cuento vierte.
Mi corazón te ofrezco.

'You seek love, false widow? You seek a love that I wish you may find.'

'The sky's little stars are my longing, where shall I find my lover, living and dying?'

'He lies dead in the water, maid of snow, covered with nostalgia and carnations.'

'Alas!, knight-errant of the cypresses, a moonlit night my soul offers you.'

'Oh, dreaming Isis! Maid without sweetness, in the mouth of children rendering her tale. I offer you my heart. Tender heart,

Corazón tenue,
herido por los ojos
de las mujeres.»

«Caballero galante,
con Dios te quedes.
Voy a buscar al conde
de los Laureles . . .»

«Adiós, mi doncellita,
rosa durmiente,
tú vas para el amor
y yo a la muerte.»

Esquilones de plata
llevan los bueyes.

Mi corazón desangra
como una fuente.

LA BALADA DEL AGUA DEL MAR

EL mar
sonríe a lo lejos.

wounded by the eyes of women.'

'Gallant knight, God be with you. I will go in search of the Count of the Laurels.'

'Farewell, sweet maid, sleeping rose, towards love you go, and I towards death.'

The oxen wear large silver bells.

My heart bleeds like a fountain.

Ballad of the Sea-water

THE sea smiles in the distance. Teeth of foam, lips of heaven.

Dientes de espuma,
labios de cielo.

«¿Qué vendes, oh joven turbia
con los senos al aire?»

«Vendo, señor, el agua
de los mares.»

«¿Qué llevas, oh negro joven,
mezclado con tu sangre?»

«Llevo, señor, el agua
de los mares.»

«Esas lágrimas salobres
¿de dónde vienen, madre?»

«Lloro, señor, el agua
de los mares.»

«Corazón, y esta amargura
seria, ¿de dónde nace?»

«¡Amarga mucho el agua
de los mares!»

'What do you sell, oh troubled girl, with your breasts bare?'
'I sell, sir, the water of the seas.
'What do you carry, oh dark youth, mixed with your blood?'
'I carry, sir, the water of the seas.'
'These salty tears, mother, where do they come from?'
'I weep, sir, the water of the seas.'
'Heart, and this grave bitterness, where does it spring from?'
'The water of the seas is very bitter!'

El mar
sonríe a lo lejos.
Dientes de espuma,
labios de cielo.

SUEÑO

MI corazón reposa junto a la fuente fría.
    (Llénala con tus hilos,
    araña del olvido.)

El agua de la fuente su canción le decía.
    (Llénala con tus hilos,
    araña del olvido.)

Mi corazón despierto sus amores decía.
    (Araña del silencio,
    téjele tu misterio.)

El agua de la fuente lo escuchaba sombría.
    (Araña del silencio,
    téjele tu misterio.)

The sea smiles in the distance, teeth of foam, lips of heaven.

Dream

MY heart rests by the cool fountain. (Fill it with your threads, spider of oblivion.)

To it the water of the fountain sang its song. (Fill it with your threads, spider of oblivion.)

My awakened heart sang its loves. (Spider of silence, weave your mystery.)

The water of the fountain listened sombrely. (Spider of silence, weave your mystery.)

Mi corazón se vuelca sobre la fuente fría.
      (Manos blancas, lejanas,
        detened a las aguas.)

Y el agua se lo lleva cantando de alegría.
      (¡Manos blancas, lejanas,
        nada queda en las aguas!)

CANTOS NUEVOS

Dice la tarde: «¡Tengo sed de sombra!»
Dice la luna: «Yo, sed de luceros.»
La fuente cristalina pide labios
y suspiros el viento.

    Yo tengo sed de aromas y de risas,
sed de cantares nuevos
sin lunas y sin lirios,
y sin amores muertos.

    Un cantar de mañana que estremezca
a los remansos quietos

My heart tumbles into the cool fountain. (White hands, faraway, halt the waters.)

And the water takes it away singing with joy. (White hands, far away, nothing remains in the water!)

New Songs

The afternoon says: 'I thirst for a shadow!' The moon says: 'I thirst for bright stars!' The crystal clear fountain asks for lips, and the wind for sighs.

I thirst for fragrance and laughs, I thirst for new songs free of moons or lilies, and free of withered amours.

A song of tomorrow that will agitate the tranquil waters of the

del porvenir. Y llene de esperanza
sus ondas y sus cienos.

Un cantar luminoso y reposado
pleno de pensamiento,
virginal de tristezas y de angustias
y virginal de ensueños.

Cantar sin carne lírica que llene
de risas el silencio
(una bandada de palomas ciegas
lanzadas al misterio).

Cantar que vaya al alma de las cosas
y al alma de los vientos
y que descanse al fin en la alegría
del corazón eterno.

DESEO

SÓLO tu corazón caliente,
y nada más.

future. And will fill with hope its ripples and its slime.

A resplendent and tempered song, rich with thought, pure of regrets or anguish, and pure of fanciful dreams.

Song without lyrical flesh filling silence with laughs (a flight of blinded pigeons thrown against the unknown).

A song reaching the spirit of things, and the spirit of the winds, a song finally resting in the joy of the eternal heart.

Wish

ONLY your warm heart, and no more.

Mi paraíso un campo
sin ruiseñor
ni liras,
con un río discreto
y una fuentecilla.

Sin la espuela del viento
sobre la fronda,
ni la estrella que quiere
ser hoja.

Una enorme luz
que fuera
luciérnaga
de otra,
en un campo de miradas rotas.

Un reposo claro
y allí nuestros besos,
lunares sonoros
del eco,
se abrirían muy lejos.

Y tu corazón caliente,
nada más.

My paradise a field without nightingale or lyre, with a discreet
river and a small fountain.
Without the spur of the wind over the foliage, without the star
wanting to be a leaf.
A great light which would be glow-worm of another, in a field
of broken glances.
A serene rest, where our kisses, resonant specks of the echo,
would open far away.
And your warm heart, no more.

BALADILLA DE LOS TRES RÍOS

EL río Guadalquivir
va entre naranjos y olivos.
Los dos ríos de Granada
bajan de la nieve al trigo.

¡Ay, amor
que se fué y no vino!

El río Guadalquivir
tiene las barbas granates.
Los dos ríos de Granada,
uno llanto y otro sangre.

¡Ay, amor
que se fué por el aire!

Para los barcos de vela
Sevilla tiene un camino;
por el agua de Granada
sólo reman los suspiros.

¡Ay, amor
que se fué y no vino!

Little Ballad of the Three Rivers

THE River Guadalquivir flows between orange- and olive-trees.
The two rivers of Granada fall from the snow to the wheat.

Ah, love that fled and never returned!

The River Guadalquivir has a garnet-coloured beard. The two
rivers of Granada, one lament and the other blood.

Ah, love that fled through the air!

For the boats with sails Seville has a path; through the waters of
Granada only sighs go rowing.

Ah, love that fled and never returned!

Guadalquivir, alta torre
y viento en los naranjales.
Dauro y Genil, torrecillas
muertas sobre los estanques.

¡Ay, amor
que se fué por el aire!

¡Quién dirá que el agua lleva
un fuego fatuo de gritos!

¡Ay, amor
que se fué y no vino!

Lleva azahar, lleva olivas,
Andalucía, a tus mares.

¡Ay, amor
que se fué por el aire!

PAISAJE

E<small>L</small> campo
de olivos
se abre, y se cierra

Guadalquivir, lofty tower and wind in the orange groves. Dauro
and Genil, little towers dead above the ponds.
   Ah, love that fled through the air!
   Who will say that the water carries a will-o'-the-wisp of cries!
   Ah, love that fled and never returned!
   Andalusia, take orange blossom, take olives, to your seas.
   Ah, love that fled through the air!

Landscape

T<small>HE</small> field of olive-trees opens and shuts like a fan. Over the olive-

como un abanico.
Sobre el olivar
hay un cielo hundido
y una lluvia oscura
de luceros fríos.
Tiembla junco y penumbra
a la orilla del río.
Se riza el aire gris.
Los olivos,
están cargados
de gritos.
Una bandada
de pájaros cautivos,
que mueven sus larguísimas
colas en lo sombrío.

LA GUITARRA

EMPIEZA el llanto
de la guitarra.
Se rompen las copas
de la madrugada.
Empieza el llanto
de la guitarra.
Es inútil callarla.

grove is a deep sky and a dark rain of cold stars. By the river bank, reeds and darkness tremble. The grey air ripples. The olive-trees are full of shrieks. A flock of captive birds that move their very long tails in the shadow.

The Guitar

THE lament of the guitar begins. The rim of dawn breaks through. The lament of the guitar begins. It is useless to hush it. It is impossible

Es imposible
callarla.
Llora monótona
como llora el agua,
como llora el viento
sobre la nevada.
Es imposible
callarla.
Llora por cosas
lejanas.
Arena del Sur caliente
que pide camelias blancas.
Llora flecha sin blanco,
la tarde sin mañana,
y el primer pájaro muerto
sobre la rama.
¡Oh, guitarra!
Corazón malherido
por cinco espadas.

PUEBLO

Sobre el monte pelado
un calvario.
Agua clara
y olivos centenarios.

to hush it. It weeps monotonous as the water weeps, as the wind weeps over the snowfall. It is impossible to hush it. It weeps for things far away. Sand of the warm South, asking for white camellias. It weeps arrow without target, evening without morning, and the first dead bird upon the branch. Oh, guitar! Heart grievously wounded by five swords.

Village

On the bare mountain a calvary. Clear water and ancient olive-trees.

Por las callejas
hombres embozados,
y en las torres
veletas girando.
Eternamente
girando.
¡Oh pueblo perdido,
en la Andalucía del llanto!

PASO

Virgen con miriñaque,
virgen de la Soledad,
abierta como un inmenso
tulipán.
En tu barco de luces
vas
por la alta marea
de la ciudad,
entre saetas turbias
y estrellas de cristal.
Virgen con miriñaque,

Through the narrow streets cloaked men, and on the towers vanes rotating. Eternally rotating. O lost village in the Andalusia of the lament!

*Paso**

Virgin in a crinoline, Virgin of the Solitude, spread like an immense tulip. In your ship of light you go through the high tide of the city, among turbulent *saetas*† and stars of crystal. Virgin in a crinoline,

---

* An image, or group of images, representing a scene from the Passion of Christ, carried in procession during Holy Week, particularly in Andalusia.

tú vas
por el río de la calle,
¡hasta el mar!

CAMINO

Cien jinetes enlutados,
¿dónde irán,
por el cielo yacente
del naranjal?
Ni a Córdoba ni a Sevilla
llegarán.
Ni a Granada la que suspira
por el mar.
Esos caballos soñolientos
los llevarán
al laberinto de las cruces
donde tiembla el cantar.
Con siete ayes clavados,
¿dónde irán
los cien jinetes andaluces
del naranjal?

you go through the river of the street, down to the sea!

Journey

One hundred horsemen in mourning, where would they go, along
the low-lying sky of the orange grove? They will neither arrive at
Córdoba nor at Seville. Nor at Granada always sighing for the sea.
Those somnolent horses will take them to the labyrinth of the cross-
es where the song trembles. With seven nailed sorrows, where would
they go, the hundred Andalusian horsemen of the orange grove?

---

† Short religious ballad sung, often spontaneously, in a religious proces-
sion.

LA LOLA

Bajo el naranjo lava
pañales de algodón.
Tiene verdes los ojos
y violeta la voz.

　　¡Ay, amor,
bajo el naranjo en flor!

El agua de la acequia
iba llena de sol,
en el olivarito
cantaba un gorrión.

　　¡Ay, amor,
bajo el naranjo en flor!

　　Luego, cuando la Lola
gaste todo el jabón,
vendrán los torerillos.

　　¡Ay, amor,
bajo el naranjo en flor!

Lola

Under the orange-tree she washes cotton swaddling-clothes. Her eyes are green, and violet is her voice.

　Ah! Love, under the orange-tree in blossom!

　The water-course flowed with sun, in the little olive-tree chirped a sparrow.

　Ah! Love, under the orange-tree in blossom!

　Later, when Lola has finished all the soap, the young bull-fighters will come.

　Ah! Love, under the orange-tree in blossom!

MALAGUEÑA

La muerte
entra y sale
de la taberna.

Pasan caballos negros
y gente siniestra
por los hondos caminos.
de la guitarra.

Y hay un olor a sal
y a sangre de hembra
en los nardos febriles
de la marina.

La muerte
entra y sale,
y sale y entra
la muerte
de la taberna.

Malagueña ★

Death goes in and out of the tavern.

Black horses and villainous people move along the deep paths of the guitar.

And there is a smell of salt and woman's blood in the feverish tuberoses of the sea-shore.

Death goes in and out, and out and in goes the death of the tavern.

★ Popular dance and tune similar to the fandango.

CANCIÓN DE JINETE

(1860)

En la luna negra
de los bandoleros,
cantan las espuelas.

Caballito negro.
¿Dónde llevas tu jinete muerto?

. . . Las duras espuelas
del bandido inmóvil
que perdió las riendas.

Caballito frío.
¡Qué perfume de flor de cuchillo!

En la luna negra,
sangraba el costado
de Sierra Morena.

Caballito negro.
¿Dónde llevas tu jinete muerto?

La noche espolea
sus negros ijares
clavándose estrellas.

Song of the Rider (1860)

In the black moon of the highwaymen the spurs sing.
Little black horse. Where are you taking your dead rider?
. . . The hard spurs of the motionless bandit who lost his reins.
Little cold horse. What a scent of knife-blossom!
In the black moon bled the mountain-side of Sierra Morena.
Little black horse. Where are you taking your dead rider?
The night spurs her black flanks pricking herself with stars.

48

Caballito frío.
¡Qué perfume de flor de cuchillo!

En la luna negra,
¡un grito! y el cuerno
largo de la hoguera.

Caballito negro.
¿Dónde llevas tu jinete muerto?

CANCIÓN DE JINETE

CÓRDOBA.
Lejana y sola.

Jaca negra, luna grande,
y aceitunas en mi alforja.
Aunque sepa los caminos
yo nunca llegaré a Córdoba.

Por el llano, por el viento,
jaca negra, luna roja.
La muerte me está mirando
desde las torres de Córdoba.

Little cold horse. What a scent of knife-blossom!
In the black moon, a shriek! and the long horn of the bonfire.
Little black horse. Where are you taking your dead rider?

Song of the Rider

CÓRDOBA. Remote and alone.

Black pony, large moon, and olives in my saddle-bag. Although I know the trail, I'll never reach Córdoba.

Through the plain, though the wind, black pony, red moon. Death is watching me from the towers of Córdoba.

¡Ay qué camino tan largo!
¡Ay mi jaca valerosa!
¡Ay que la muerte me espera,
antes de llegar a Córdoba!

Córdoba.
Lejana y sola.

ES VERDAD

¡Ay qué trabajo me cuesta
quererte como te quiero!

Por tu amor me duele el aire,
el corazón
y el sombrero.

¿Quién me compraría a mí,
este cintillo que tengo
y esta tristeza de hilo
blanco, para hacer pañuelos?

¡Ay qué trabajo me cuesta
quererte como te quiero!

Ah! How long the road! Ah! My brave pony! Ah! Death waits for
me before I reach Córdoba!
    Córdoba. Remote and alone.

It is True

OH, how hard it is to love you as I do!
    Because of your love, the air, my heart and my hat hurt me.
    Who would buy this ribbon of mine and this sadness of white
cotton, to make handkerchiefs with?
    Oh, how hard it is to love you as I do!

CANCIÓN

La niña de bello rostro
está cogiendo aceituna.
El viento, galán de torres,
la prende por la cintura.
Pasaron cuatro jinetes,
sobre jacas andaluzas
con trajes de azul y verde,
con largas capas oscuras.
«Vente a Córdoba, muchacha.»
La niña no los escucha.
Pasaron tres torerillos
delgaditos de cintura,
con trajes color naranja
y espadas de plata antigua.
«Vente a Sevilla, muchacha.»
La niña no los escucha.
Cuando la tarde se puso
morada, con luz difusa,
pasó un joven que llevaba
rosas y mirtos de luna.
«Vente a Granada, muchacha.»
Y la niña no lo escucha.
La niña del bello rostro
sigue cogiendo aceituna,

Song

The girl with the beautiful face is gathering olives. The wind, that suitor of towers, takes her by the waist. Four riders passed on Andalusian ponies, with suits of blue and green, with long dark cloaks. 'Come to Córdoba, lass.' The girl pays no heed. Three young bull-fighters passed, of slender waist, with orange-coloured suits and swords of antique silver. 'Come to Seville, lass.' The girl pays no heed. When the evening became purple, with diffused light, a youth passed by bringing roses and myrtle of the moon. 'Come to Granada, lass.' But the girl pays no heed. The girl with the beautiful

con el brazo gris del viento
ceñido por la cintura.

LA LUNA ASOMA

Cuando sale la luna
se pierden las campanas
y aparecen las sendas
impenetrables.

Cuando sale la luna,
el mar cubre la tierra
y el corazón se siente
isla en el infinito.

Nadie come naranjas
bajo la luna llena.
Es preciso comer
fruta verde y helada.

Cuando sale la luna
de cien rostros iguales,
la moneda de plata
solloza en el bolsillo.

face goes on gathering olives, with the grey arm of the wind encircling her waist.

The Moon Appears

When the moon comes out, the bells fade away, and the impenetrable paths appear.

When the moon comes out, the sea covers the earth, and the heart feels like an island in the infinite.

No one eats oranges under the full moon. One must eat green and icy fruit.

When the moon of one hundred identical faces comes out, the silver coins in the pocket sob.

SERENATA

(Homenaje a Lope de Vega)

POR las orillas del río
se está la noche mojando
y en los pechos de Lolita
se mueren de amor los ramos.

Se mueren de amor los ramos.

La noche canta desnuda
sobre los puentes de marzo.
Lolita lava su cuerpo
con agua salobre y nardos.

Se mueren de amor los ramos.

La noche de anís y plata
relumbra por los tejados.
Plata de arroyos y espejos.
Anís de tus muslos blancos.

Se mueren de amor los ramos.

Serenata
(Homage to Lope de Vega)

ALONG the river shore the night steeps itself, and in the breasts of Lolita the branches die of love.

The branches die of love.

The night sings naked above the bridges of March. Lolita bathes her body with salt water and tuberoses.

The branches die of love.

The *anís** and silver night shines over the roof-tops. Silver of rivulets and looking-glasses. *Anís* of your white thighs.

The branches die of love.

---

* A Spanish aniseed liqueur.

EL NIÑO MUDO

El niño busca su voz.
(La tenía el rey de los grillos.)
En una gota de agua
buscaba su voz el niño.

No la quiero para hablar;
me haré con ella un anillo
que llevará mi silencio
en su dedo pequeñito.

En una gota de agua
buscaba su voz el niño.

(La voz cautiva, a lo lejos,
se ponía un traje de grillo.)

DESPEDIDA

Si muero,
dejad el balcón abierto.

The Dumb Child

The child is searching for his voice. (The king of the crickets had it.) In a drop of water the child was searching for his voice.

I do not want it to speak with; I shall make with it a ring that my silence will wear on its little finger.

In a drop of water the child was searching for his voice.

(The captive voice, in the distance, was putting on the garb of a cricket.)

Farewell

If I die, leave the balcony open.

El niño come naranjas.
(Desde mi balcón lo veo.)

El segador siega el trigo.
(Desde mi balcón lo siento.)

¡Si muero,
dejad el balcón abierto!

SUICIDIO

(Quizás fué por no saberte la Geometría)

EL jovencillo se olvidaba.
Eran las diez de la mañana.

Su corazón se iba llenando
de alas rotas y flores de trapo.

Notó que ya no le quedaba
en la boca más que una palabra.

Y al quitarse los guantes, caía,
de sus manos, suave ceniza.

The child eats oranges. (From my balcony I see him.)
The harvester scythes the corn. (From my balcony I hear him.)
If I die, leave the balcony open!

Suicide
(Perhaps it happened because you did not know your geometry)

THE lad was losing consciousness. It was ten in the morning.
His heart was filling with broken wings and rag-flowers.
He felt that only one word remained in his mouth.
And on taking off his gloves, soft ashes fell from his hands.

Por el balcón se veía una torre.
Él se sintió balcón y torre.

Vió, sin duda, cómo le miraba
el reloj detenido en su caja.

Vió su sombra tendida y quieta,
en el blanco diván de seda.

Y el joven rígido, geométrico,
con un hacha rompió el espejo.

Al romperlo, un gran chorro de sombra,
inundó la quimérica alcoba.

GRANADA Y 1850

Desde un cuarto
oigo el surtidor.

Un dedo de la parra
y un rayo de sol.

Through the balcony window a tower was visible. He felt himself window and tower.

He saw, no doubt, how the clock motionless in its box watched him.

He saw his quiet and reclining shadow on the white silk divan.

And the rigid, geometrical lad with a hatchet shattered the mirror.

On shattering it, a great jet of shadow invaded the unreal alcove.

Granada and 1850

From my room I hear the fountain.

A vine-tendril and a ray of sunshine. They point at the place of

Señalan hacia el sitio
de mi corazón.

Por el aire de agosto
se van las nubes. Yo,
sueño que no sueño
dentro del surtidor.

CANCIÓN DEL NARANJO SECO

LEÑADOR.
Córtame la sombra.
Líbrame del suplicio
de verme sin toronjas.

¿Por qué nací entre espejos?
El día me da vueltas.
Y la noche me copia
en todas sus estrellas.

Quiero vivir sin verme.
Y hormigas y vilanos,
soñaré que son mis
hojas y mis pájaros.

my heart.

Through the August air the clouds drift. And I dream that I do
not dream within the fountain.

Song of the Withered Orange-tree

WOODCUTTER. Cut my shadow. Deliver me from the torture of
beholding myself fruitless.

Why was I born surrounded by mirrors? The day turns round
me. And the night reproduces me in each of her stars.

I want to live without seeing myself. And I shall dream that ants
and hawks are my leaves and birds.

Leñador.
Córtame la sombra.
Líbrame del suplicio
de verme sin toronjas.

ROMANCE DE LA TALABARTERA

En un cortijo de Córdoba,
entre jarales y adelfas,
vivía un talabartero
con una talabartera.
Ella era mujer arisca,
él hombre de gran paciencia,
ella giraba en los veinte
y él pasaba de cincuenta.
¡Santo Dios, cómo reñían!
Miren ustedes la fiera,
burlando al débil marido
con los ojos y la lengua.
Cabellos de emperadora
tiene la talabartera,

Woodcutter. Cut my shadow. Deliver me from the torture of beholding myself fruitless.

Ballad of the Saddler's Wife ★

In a farmstead of Córdoba there lived among rock-roses and rose-bays, a saddler and his wife. She was a churlish woman, he a man of great patience. She was in her twenties and he beyond fifty. God Almighty, how they quarrelled! Gentlemen, look at the shrew, poking fun at her feeble husband with her eyes and her tongue. The hair

---

★ This ballad in Lorca's play *La zapatera prodigiosa* (The Shoemaker's Prodigious Wife) is told by the shoemaker, disguised as a ballad pedlar, while pointing with a rod at the outspread illustrated ballad. It is directed at his frivolous wife, who is in the audience.

y una carne como el agua
cristalina de Lucena.
Cuando movía las faldas
en tiempos de Primavera
olía toda su ropa
a limón y a yerbabuena.
¡Ay, qué limón, limón
de la limonera!
¡Qué apetitosa
talabartera!
Ved cómo la cortejaban
mocitos de gran presencia
en caballos relucientes
llenos de borlas de seda.
Gente cabal y garbosa
que pasaba por la puerta
haciendo brillar, adrede,
las onzas de sus cadenas.
La conversación a todos
daba la talabartera,
y ellos caracoleaban
sus jacas sobre las piedras.
Miradla hablando con uno
bien peinada y bien compuesta,
mientras el pobre marido
clava en el cuero la lezna.

of an empress this saddler's wife had, and flesh like the dear water of
Lucena. When she swayed her skirts in springtime, all her clothes
smelt of lemon and mint. Ah, what a lemon, lemon of the lemon-
girl! What a desirable saddler's wife! See how they wooed her, young
men of great presence mounted on shining horses covered with silk
tassels. Respectable and grand people who went by her door, pur-
posely flicking and flashing the gold ounces on their waist-chains.
The saddler's wife conversed with all, while they caracolled their
ponies on the cobble-stones. Look at her talking to someone, well
combed and truly composed, while her poor husband drives the

Esposo viejo y decente
casado con joven tierna,
¡qué tunante caballista
roba tu amor en la puerta!
Un lunes por la mañana
a eso de las once y media,
cuando el sol deja sin sombra
los juncos y madreselvas,
cuando alegremente bailan
brisa y tomillo en la sierra
y van cayendo las verdes
hojas de las madroñeras,
regaba sus alhelíes
la arisca talabartera.
Llegó su amigo trotando
una jaca cordobesa
y le dijo entre suspiros:
«Niña, si tú lo quisieras,
cenaríamos mañana
los dos solos, en tu mesa.»
«¿Y qué harás de mi marido?»
«Tu marido no se entera.»
«¿Qué piensas hacer?» «Matarlo.»
«Es ágil. Quizá no puedas.
¿Tienes revólver?» «¡Mejor!

bodkin through the leather. Venerable and decent husband married
to a young girl, what rascal of a horseman steals your love at the
door? On a Monday morning, about half past eleven, when the sun
leaves the rushes and the honey-suckle shadowless, when joyfully
breeze and thyme dance on the hills, and the green leaves of the
madroño-trees fall, the churlish saddler's wife was watering her
wallflowers. Her friend arrived trotting on a Cordovan pony, and in
between sighs said to her: 'Girl, if you wish, tomorrow we could sup
by ourselves, just the two of us, at your table.' 'And what will you do
with my husband?' 'Your husband will be none the wiser.' 'What is
in your mind?' 'To kill him.' 'He is quick. Perhaps you can't. Have

¡Tengo navaja barbera!»
«¿Corta mucho?» «Más que el frío.
Y no tiene ni una mella.»
«¿No has mentido?» «Le daré.
diez puñaladas certeras
en esta disposición,
que me parece estupenda:
cuatro en la región lumbar,
una en la tetilla izquierda,
otra en semejante sitio
y dos en cada cadera.»
«¿Lo matarás en seguida?»
«Esta noche cuando vuelva
con el cuero y con las crines
por la curva de la acequia.»

(*La Zapatera Prodigiosa*, Acto II)

ROMANCE DE LA LUNA, LUNA

LA luna vino a la fragua
con su polisón de nardos.
El niño la mira, mira.
El niño la está mirando.

you a revolver?' 'Far better! I have a barber's razor!' 'Does it cut?'
'More than the frost. And it has not a jag.' 'You are not lying?' 'I'll
give him ten well-aimed stabs, in this manner, which I think fine:
four in the lumbar region, one in the left nipple, another in a simi-
lar place, and two in each buttock.' 'Will you kill him at once?'
'Tonight, when he returns with the leather and the horsehair, by the
bend beside the water-course.'

Ballad of the Moon, Moon

THE moon comes to the smithy in her tuberose crinoline. The child
looks and looks at her. The child is looking at her. In the agitated

En el aire conmovido
mueve la luna sus brazos
y enseña, lúbrica y pura,
sus senos de duro estaño.
«Huye luna, luna, luna.
Si vinieran los gitanos,
harían con tu corazón
collares y anillos blancos.»
«Niño, déjame que baile.
Cuando vengan los gitanos,
te encontrarán sobre el yunque
con los ojillos cerrados.»
«Huye luna, luna, luna,
que ya siento sus caballos.»
«Niño, déjame, no pises
mi blancor almidonado.»

El jinete se acercaba
tocando el tambor del llano.
Dentro de la fragua el niño
tiene los ojos cerrados.

Por el olivar venían,
bronce y sueño, los gitanos.

air the moon moves her arms and discloses, voluptuous, pure, her breasts of hard tin. Run away moon, moon, moon. 'If the gipsies should come, they will make of your heart necklaces and white rings.' 'Child, let me dance. When the gipsies come, they will find you on the anvil with your little eyes closed.' 'Run away moon, moon, moon, for I hear now their horses.' 'Child, leave me, do not step on my starched whiteness.'

Drumming the plain, the horseman was coming near. Inside the smithy the child has closed his eyes.

Along the olive grove the gipsies were coming, bronze and dream. Heads high and eyes half-closed.

Las cabezas levantadas
y los ojos entornados.

Cómo canta la zumaya,
¡ay, cómo canta en el árbol!
Por el cielo va la luna
con un niño de la mano.

Dentro de la fragua lloran
dando gritos, los gitanos.
El aire la vela, vela.
El aire la está velando.

REYERTA

En la mitad del barranco
las navajas de Albacete,
bellas de sangre contraria,
relucen como los peces.
Una dura luz de naipe
recorta en el agrio verde
caballos enfurecidos
y perfiles de jinetes.
En la copa de un olivo
lloran dos viejas mujeres.

How the owl hoots! Ah, how it hoots in the tree! Through the sky goes the moon holding a child by the hand.

Inside the smithy the gipsies shout and weep. The breeze watches over it, watches. The breeze is watching over it.

The Fight

In the midst of the ravine the opened Albacete clasp-knives, rendered beautiful with enemy's blood, glinted like fishes. A hard playing-card light outlines in the sharp green, enraged horses and the profiles of horsemen. On the branches of an olive-tree two old

El toro de la reyerta
se sube por las paredes.
Ángeles negros traían
pañuelos y agua de nieve.
Ángeles con grandes alas
de navajas de Albacete.
Juan Antonio el de Montilla
rueda muerto la pendiente,
su cuerpo lleno de lirios
y una granada en las sienes.
Ahora monta cruz de fuego,
carretera de la muerte.

★

El juez, con guardia civil,
por los olivares viene.
Sangre resbalada gime
muda canción de serpiente.
«Señores guardias civiles:
aquí pasó lo de siempre.
Han muerto cuarto romanos
y cinco cartagineses.»

★

La tarde loca de higueras
y de rumores calientes

women weep. The bull of the fight is climbing the walls. Black angels brought handkerchiefs and melted snow. Angels with large wings of Albacete blades. Juan Antonio from Montilla rolls down the slope dead, his body laden with lilies and a pomegranate on his brow. Now he rides a cross of fire on the highway to death.

The judge, and Civil Guards, come along the olive grove. The trailed blood moans a silent snake song. 'Gentlemen of the Civil Guard: Here we have the same old story. Four Romans and five Carthaginians have died.'

The afternoon, delirious with fig-trees and warm murmurs,

cae desmayada en los muslos
heridos de los jinetes.
Y ángeles negros volaban
por el aire del poniente.
Ángeles de largas trenzas
y corazones de aceite.

ROMANCE SONÁMBULO

VERDE que te quiero verde.
Verde viento. Verdes ramas.
El barco sobre la mar
y el caballo en la montaña.
Con la sombra en la cintura
ella sueña en su baranda,
verde carne, pelo verde,
con ojos de fría plata.
Verde que te quiero verde.
Bajo la luna gitana,
las cosas la están mirando
y ella no puede mirarlas.

★

faints on the wounded thighs of the horsemen. And black angels
were flying through the air of the setting sun. Angels of long tress-
es and hearts of olive-oil.

Somnambular Ballad

GREEN, I want you green. Green wind. Green branches. The ship
upon the sea and the horse on the mountain. With the shadow at
her waist she dreams on her balcony, green flesh, green hair, and eyes
of cold silver. Green, I want you green. Beneath the gipsy moon,
things are looking at her, things she cannot see.

Verde que te quiero verde.
Grandes estrellas de escarcha
vienen con el pez de sombra
que abre el camino del alba.
La higuera frota su viento
con la lija de sus ramas,
y el monte, gato garduño,
eriza sus pitas agrias.
¿Pero quién vendrá? ¿Y por dónde...?
Ella sigue en su baranda,
verde carne, pelo verde,
soñando en la mar amarga.

★

«Compadre, quiero cambiar
mi caballo por su casa,
mi montura por su espejo,
mi cuchillo por su manta.
Compadre, vengo sangrando,
desde los puertos de Cabra.»
«Si yo pudiera, mocito,
este trato se cerraba.
Pero yo ya no soy yo,
ni mi casa es ya mi casa.»
«Compadre, quiero morir

Green, I want you green. Great stars of white frost come with the fish of darkness that opens the way for the daybreak. The fig-tree rubs its air with the sandpaper of its leaves, and the mountain, like a thieving cat, bristles its sour agaves. But who will come? And from where? She lingers on her balcony, green flesh, green hair, dreaming of the bitter sea.

'Friend, I want to change my horse for your house, my saddle for your looking-glass, my knife for your rug. Friend, I have come bleeding from the passes of Cabra.' 'If I could, young man, this bargain would be closed. But I am no longer I, nor is my house now

decentemente en mi cama.
De acero, si puede ser,
con las sábanas de holanda.
¿No ves la herida que tengo
desde el pecho a la garganta?»
«Trescientas rosas morenas
lleva tu pechera blanca.
Tu sangre rezuma y huele
alrededor de tu faja.
Pero yo ya no soy yo,
ni mi casa es ya mi casa.»
«Dejadme subir al menos
hasta las altas barandas,
¡dejadme subir!, dejadme,
hasta las verdes barandas.
Barandales de la luna
por donde retumba el agua.»

      ★

Ya suben los dos compadres
hacia las altas barandas.
Dejando un rastro de sangre.
Dejando un rastro de lágrimas.
Temblaban en los tejados
farolillos de hojalata.

my house.' 'Friend, I want to die decently in my bed. Made of steel,
if possible, with sheets of fine Holland. Do you not see the wound
I have from my breast to my throat?' 'The white front of your shirt
bears three hundred dark roses. Your blood is pungent and oozes
around your sash. But I am no longer I, nor is my house now my
house.' 'Let me climb at least up to the high balustrades; let me climb
up!, let me, up to the green balustrades. Multiple balustrades of the
moon where water resounds.'

    Now the two friends climb up to the high balustrades. Leaving
a trail of blood. Leaving a trail of tears. Small tin lanterns trembled

Mil panderos de cristal
herían la madrugada.

★

Verde que te quiero verde,
verde viento, verdes ramas.
Los dos compadres subieron.
El largo viento dejaba
en la boca un raro gusto
de hiel, de menta y de albahaca.
«¡Compadre! ¿Dónde está, dime,
dónde está tu niña amarga?
¡Cuántas veces te esperó!
¡Cuántas veces te esperara,
cara fresca, negro pelo,
en esta verde baranda!»

★

Sobre el rostro del aljibe
se mecía la gitana.
Verde carne, pelo verde,
con ojos de fría plata.
Un carámbano de luna
la sostiene sobre el agua.
La noche se puso íntima

on the roofs. A thousand glass tambourines wounded the daybreak.

Green, I want you green, green wind, green branches. The two friends climbed up. The full wind left in the mouth a strange taste of gall, of mint, and of sweet-basil. 'Friend! Where is she, tell me, where is your bitter girl? How often she waited for you! How often she would wait for you, cool face, black hair, on this green balustrade!'

Over the face of the cistern the gipsy girl rocked. Green flesh, green hair, and eyes of cold silver. An icicle of moon holds her above the water. The night became as intimate as a little square. Drunken

como una pequeña plaza.
Guardias civiles borrachos
en la puerta golpeaban.
Verde que te quiero verde.
Verde viento. Verdes ramas.
El barco sobre la mar.
Y el caballo en la montaña.

LA MONJA GITANA

SILENCIO de cal y mirto.
Malvas en las hierbas finas.
La monja borda alhelíes
sobre una tela pajiza.
Vuelan en la araña gris
siete pájaros del prisma.
La iglesia gruñe a lo lejos
como un oso panza arriba.
¡Qué bien borda! ¡Con qué gracia!
Sobre la tela pajiza
ella quisiera bordar
flores de su fantasía.
¡Qué girasol! ¡Qué magnolia

Civil Guards were banging at the door. Green, I want you green. Green wind. Green branches. The ship upon the sea. And the horse on the mountain.

The Gipsy Nun

SILENCE of lime and myrtle. Wild mallows among the flowering reeds. The nun embroiders wallflowers on a straw-coloured cloth. In the grey chandelier fly seven birds of the prism. The church growls in the distance like a bear on its back. How well she embroiders! How daintily! On the pale-yellow cloth she would like to embroider flowers of her fancy. What a sunflower! What a magnolia of spangles

de lentejuelas y cintas!
¡Qué azafranes y qué lunas
en el mantel de la misa!
Cinco toronjas se endulzan
en la cercana cocina.
Las cinco llagas de Cristo
cortadas en Almería.
Por los ojos de la monja
galopan dos caballistas.
Un rumor último y sordo
le despega la camisa,
y al mirar nubes y montes
en las yertas lejanías,
se quiebra su corazón
de azúcar y yerbaluisa.
¡Oh, qué llanura empinada
con veinte soles arriba!
¡Qué ríos puestos de pie
vislumbra su fantasía!
Pero sigue con sus flores,
mientras que de pie, en la brisa,
la luz juega el ajedrez
alto de la celosía.

and ribbons! What saffrons and what moons on the altar-cloth! Five citrons are sweetening in the nearby kitchen. The five nasturtiums★ cut in Almería. Through the nun's eyes gallop two highwaymen. An ultimate and dormant murmur lifts her camisole, and as she looks towards the clouds and hills in the desolate remoteness, her sugar and verbena heart breaks. Oh, what a lofty plain, with twenty suns above! What upstanding rivers does her fantasy visualize! But she proceeds with her flowers while in the breeze the vertical light plays on the lofty chequers of the lattice-window.

★ *Llagas de cristo*, literally 'wounds of Christ', is the common Spanish name for the common garden 'nasturtium'. The word-play probably derives from the stains on the five-petalled flower.

LA CASADA INFIEL

Y QUE yo me la llevé al río
creyendo que era mozuela,
pero tenía marido.
Fué la noche de Santiago
y casi por compromiso.
Se apagaron los faroles
y se encendieron los grillos.
En las últimas esquinas
toqué sus pechos dormidos,
y se me abrieron de pronto
como ramos de jacintos.
El almidón de su enagua
me sonaba en el oído
como una pieza de seda
rasgada por diez cuchillos.
Sin luz de plata en sus copas
los árboles han crecido,
y un horizonte de perros
ladra muy lejos del río.

★

Pasadas las zarzamoras,
los juncos y los espinos,

The Faithless Wife

AND I took her to the river believing her a maid, but she had a husband. It was on St James's night, and almost as if in duty bound. The street-lights went out and the crickets flared up. By the last street corners I touched her sleeping breasts, and they opened to me suddenly like spikes of hyacinth. The starch of her petticoat sounded in my ear like a piece of silk rent by ten knives. The trees, without silver light on their tops, have grown larger, a horizon of dogs barks very far from the river.

Past the blackberries, the reeds, and the hawthorn, underneath

71

bajo su mata de pelo
hice un hoyo sobre el limo.
Yo me quité la corbata.
Ella se quitó el vestido.
Yo, el cinturón con revólver.
Ella, sus cuatro corpiños.
Ni nardos ni caracolas
tienen el cutis tan fino,
ni los cristales con luna
relumbran con ese brillo.
Sus muslos se me escapaban
como peces sorprendidos,
la mitad llenos de lumbre,
la mitad llenos de frío.
Aquella noche corrí
el mejor de los caminos,
montado en potra de nácar
sin bridas y sin estribos.
No quiero decir, por hombre,
las cosas que ella me dijo.
La luz del entendimiento
me hace ser muy comedido.
Sucia de besos y arena,
yo me la llevé del río.
Con el aire se batían
las espadas de los lirios.

her cluster of hair I made a hollow in the fine sand. I took off my
tie. She took off her dress. I, my belt with the revolver. She, her four
bodices. Nor tuberose nor shell have skin so fine, nor do glass
mirrors shine with such brilliance. Her thighs slipped from me like
startled fish, one half full of fire, one half full of cold. That night I
galloped on the best of roads, mounted on a mother-of-pearl mare,
without bridle or stirrups. As a man, I won't repeat the things she
said to me. The light of understanding has made me most discreet.
Smeared with sand and kisses I took her away from the river. The
swords of the lilies battled with the air.

Me porté como quien soy.
Como un gitano legítimo.
La regalé un costurero
grande de raso pajizo,
y no quise enamorarme
porque teniendo marido
me dijo que era mozuela
cuando la llevaba al río.

ROMANCE DE LA PENA NEGRA

Las piquetas de los gallos
cavan buscando la aurora,
cuando por el monte oscuro
baja Soledad Montoya.
Cobre amarillo, su carne,
huele a caballo y a sombra.
Yunques ahumados, sus pechos,
gimen canciones redondas.
«Soledad, ¿por quién preguntas
sin compaña y a estas horas?»
«Pregunte por quien pregunte,
dime, ¿a ti qué se te importa?
Vengo a buscar lo que busco,
mi alegría y mi persona.»

I behaved like the person I am. Like a proper gipsy. I gave her a
large sewing basket of straw-coloured satin, and I did not want to let
myself fall in love because though she had a husband, she told me
she was a maiden as I was taking her to the river.

Ballad of the Black Sorrow

Cockerels' beaks dig in search of the dawn, when Soledad
Montoya descends the dark mountain. Her flesh like brass, smells of
horse and shadow. Her breasts like smoky anvils, wail round songs.
'Soledad, whom do you ask for, unaccompanied, at this hour?'
'Whoever I ask for, tell me: what business is it of yours? I come in

«Soledad de mis pesares,
caballo que se desboca
al fin encuentra la mar
y se lo tragan las olas.»
«No me recuerdes el mar
que la pena negra brota
en las tierras de aceituna
bajo el rumor de las hojas.»
«¡Soledad, qué pena tienes!
¡Qué pena tan lastimosa!
Lloras zumo de limón
agrio de espera y de boca.»
«¡Qué pena tan grande! Corro
mi casa como una loca,
mis dos trenzas por el suelo,
de la cocina a la alcoba.
¡Qué pena! Me estoy poniendo
de azabache carne y ropa.
¡Ay, mis camisas de hilo!
¡Ay, mis muslos de amapola!»
«Soledad: lava tu cuerpo
con agua de las alondras,
y deja tu corazón
en paz, Soledad Montoya.»

search of what I am seeking, my joy and my own self.' 'Soledad
of my sorrow, a horse that darts away ultimately meets the sea, and is
swallowed up by the waves.' 'Do not remind me of the sea, for the
black sorrow rises in the land of olives from under the murmur of
leaves.' 'Soledad, how sorrowful you are! What a pitiful sorrow! You
weep drops of lemon, sour with waiting and sour to the mouth.' 'How
great my sorrow! I pace my house like a madwoman, my two tresses
trailing the floor, from the kitchen to the bedroom. What sorrow!
My flesh and clothes are turning black like jet. Ah, my linen shifts!
Ah, my thighs of red poppy!' 'Soledad: cleanse your body with water
fresh as skylarks, and leave your heart in peace, Soledad Montoya.'

Por abajo canta el río:
volante de cielo y hojas.
Con flores de calabaza,
la nueva luz se corona.
¡Oh pena de los gitanos!
Pena limpia y siempre sola.
¡Oh pena de cauce oculto
y madrugada remota!

SAN GABRIEL

(Sevilla)

I

UN bello niño de junco,
anchos hombros, fino talle,
piel de nocturna manzana,
boca triste y ojos grandes,
nervio de plata caliente,
ronda la desierta calle.
Sus zapatos de charol
rompen las dalias del aire,
con los dos ritmos que cantan
breves lutos celestiales.

Down below the river sings: flounce of sky and leaves. With pumpkin flowers the new light crowns itself Oh, sorrow of the gipsies! Pure sorrow and always solitary. Oh, sorrow of hidden course and distant daybreak!

Saint Gabriel
(Seville)

I

A HANDSOME willowy lad, wide of shoulder, slender of waist, skin of nocturnal apple, sad mouth and large eyes, nerve of fiery silver, walks about the deserted street. His patent-leather shoes crush the

En la ribera del mar
no hay palma que se le iguale,
ni emperador coronado,
ni lucero caminante.
Cuando la cabeza inclina
sobre su pecho de jaspe,
la noche busca llanuras
porque quiere arrodillarse.
Las guitarras suenan solas
para San Gabriel Arcángel,
domador de palomillas
y enemigo de los sauces.
«San Gabriel: el niño llora
en el vientre de su madre.
No olvides que los gitanos
te regalaron el traje.»

2

Anunciación de los Reyes,
bien lunada y mal vestida,
abre la puerta al lucero
que por la calle venía.
El Arcángel San Gabriel,
entre azucena y sonrisa,

dahlias of the air, in a double cadence of brief celestial dirges. No palm leaf on the sea-shore can match him, nor a crowned emperor, nor a wandering star. When his head bends over his jasper breast, the night seeks plains because it wants to kneel. The guitars strike up alone for the Archangel Saint Gabriel, tamer of white moths and hater of sallows. 'Saint Gabriel: The child cries in his mother's belly. Don't forget the gipsies gave you the suit.'

2

Anunciación de los Reyes, moonlight dark and poorly dressed, opens the door to the star coming down the street. The Archangel Saint Gabriel, between a lily and a smile, great-grandson of the

biznieto de la Giralda,
se acercaba de visita.
En su chaleco bordado
grillos ocultos palpitan.
Las estrellas de la noche
se volvieron campanillas.
«San Gabriel: Aquí me tienes
con tres clavos de alegría.
Tu fulgor abre jazmines
sobre mi cara encendida.»
«Dios te salve, Anunciación.
Morena de maravilla.
Tendrás un niño más bello
que los tallos de la brísa.»
«¡Ay, San Gabriel de mis ojos!
¡Gabrielillo de mi vida!
Para sentarte yo sueño
un sillón de clavellinas.»
«Dios te salve, Anunciación,
bien lunada y mal vestida.
Tu niño tendrá en el pecho
un lunar y tres heridas.»
«¡Ay, San Gabriel que reluces!
¡Gabrielillo de mi vida!

Giralda,* was coming to pay a visit. In his embroidered waistcoat
hidden crickets fluttered. The stars of the night became bells. 'Saint
Gabriel, here I am with three nails of joy. Your radiance unfolds jas-
mine-flowers on my flushed face.' 'God be with you, Anunciación.
Dark girl of wonder. You will bear a child prettier than the stems of
the breeze.' 'Ah, Saint Gabriel, joy of my eyes! Little Gabriel of
mine! I dream of a chair of carnations for you to sit on.' 'God be
with you, Anunciación, moonlight dark and poorly dressed. Your
child will have on his chest a mole and three gashes.' 'Ah, resplen-
dent Saint Gabriel! Little Gabriel of mine! Deep in my breasts the

* *La Giralda*, the slender Moorish tower in Seville.

En el fondo de mis pechos
ya nace la leche tibia.»
«Dios te salve, Anunciación.
Madre de cien dinastías.
Áridos lucen tus ojos,
paisajes de caballista.»

★

El niño canta en el seno
de Anunciación sorprendida.
Tres balas de almendra verde
tiemblan en su vocecita.
Ya San Gabriel en el aire
por una escala subía.
Las estrellas de la noche
se volvieron siemprevivas.

PRENDIMIENTO DE ANTOÑITO EL CAMBORIO EN EL CAMINO DE SEVILLA

ANTONIO Torres Heredia,
hijo y nieto de Camborios,
con una vara de mimbre
va a Sevilla a ver los toros.

---

warm milk already springs.' 'God be with you, Anunciación. Mother of a hundred dynasties. Your eyes shine barren, landscapes of highwaymen.'

The child sings in the womb of startled Anunciación. Three bullets of green almond waver in his little voice.

Saint Gabriel now in the air was climbing up a ladder. The stars of the night became immortelles.

The Arrest of Antoñito el Camborio on the Way to Seville

ANTONIO Torres Heredia, son and grandson of Camborios, with a willow cane goes to Seville to see a bullfight. Swarthy from green

Moreno de verde luna,
anda despacio y garboso.
Sus empavonados bucles
le brillan entre los ojos.
A la mitad del camino
cortó limones redondos,
y los fué tirando al agua
hasta que la puso de oro.
Y a la mitad del camino,
bajo las ramas de un olmo,
guardia civil caminera
lo llevó codo con codo.

       ★

El día se va despacio,
la tarde colgada a un hombro,
dando una larga torera
sobre el mar y los arroyos.
Las aceitunas aguardan
la noche de Capricornio,
y una corta brisa, ecuestre,
salta los montes de plomo.
Antonio Torres Heredia,
hijo y nieto de Camborios,

moon he walks slow and jauntily. His lustrous locks of hair glint
between his eyes. Half-way on the journey he picked round lemons,
throwing them into the water until he turned it to gold. And half-
way on the journey, under the branches of an elm, Civil Guards on
foot took him away elbow to elbow.

The day withdraws slowly with the evening on a shoulder hung,
and makes a long pass★ over the sea and rivulets. The olives await the
Capricorn night, and a short equestrian breeze jumps the leaden hills.
Antonio Torres Heredia, son and grandson of Camborios, comes

★ A bullfighting image.

viene sin vara de mimbre
entre los cinco tricornios.

Antonio, ¿quién eres tú?
Si te llamaras Camborio,
hubieras hecho una fuente
de sangre con cinco chorros.
Ni tú eres hijo de nadie,
ni legítimo Camborio.
¡Se acabaron los gitanos
que iban por el monte solos!
Están los viejos cuchillos
tiritando bajo el polvo.

★

A las nueve de la noche
lo llevan al calabozo,
mientras los guardias civiles
beben limonada todos.
Y a las nueve de la noche
le cierran el calabozo,
mientras el cielo reluce
como la grupa de un potro.

along without willow cane between the five three-cornered hats.

Antonio, who are you? If you were a Camborio, you would have sprung a fountain of blood with five jets. You are nobody's son, nor a true Camborio. Gone are the lone gipsies who wandered through the hills! The old knives are shivering under the dust.

At nine in the evening he is taken to the jail, while all the Civil Guards drink lemonade. And at nine in the evening his cell is locked, while the sky glistens like the croup of a colt.

MUERTE DE ANTOÑITO EL CAMBORIO

Voces de muerte sonaron
cerca del Guadalquivir.
Voces antiguas que cercan
voz de clavel varonil.
Les clavó sobre las botas
mordiscos de jabalí.
En la lucha daba saltos
jabonados de delfín.
Bañó con sangre enemiga
su corbata carmesí,
pero eran cuatro puñales
y tuvo que sucumbir.
Cuando las estrellas clavan
rejones al agua gris,
cuando los erales sueñan
verónicas de alhelí,
voces de muerte sonaron
cerca del Guadalquivir.

★

Death of Antoñito el Camborio

Voices of death rang near the Guadalquivir. Ancient voices encir-
cling voice of manly carnation. He pierced their boots as with bites
of wild boar. He leapt in the fight with the smoothness of the dol-
phin. With enemy blood he stained his crimson tie, but there were
four daggers and he had to succumb. When the stars thrust javelins
into the grey water, when the yearlings dream *verónicas*★ of
wallflowers, voices of death rang near the Guadalquivir.

★ *Verónica*, a pass in bullfighting.

«Antonio Torres Heredia,
Camborio de dura crin,
moreno de verde luna,
voz de clavel varonil:
¿quién te ha quitado la vida
cerca del Guadalquivir?»
«Mis cuatro primos Heredias,
hijos de Benamejí.
Lo que en otros no envidiaban,
ya lo envidiaban en mí.
Zapatos color corinto,
medallones de marfil,
y este cutis amasado
con aceituna y jazmín.»
«¡Ay, Antoñito el Camborio,
digno de una Emperatriz!
Acuérdate de la Virgen
porque te vas a morir.»
«¡Ay, Federico García,
llama a la Guardia Civil!
Ya mi talle se ha quebrado
como caña de maíz.»

Tres golpes de sangre tuvo
y se murió de perfil.
Viva moneda que nunca

'Antonio Torres Heredia, a true Camborio, swarthy from green moon, voice of manly carnation: Who took your life away near the Guadalquivir?' 'My four Heredia cousins, sons of Benamejí. They did not envy in others what they envied in me. Raisin-coloured shoes, ivory lockets, and this skin kneaded of olive and jasmine.' 'Ah, Antoñito el Camborio, worthy of an Empress! Remember the Virgin because you are about to die.' 'Ah, Federico García, send for the Civil Guard! Already my waist has snapped like a stalk of maize.' He spurted three gushes of blood, and died in profile. Living

se volverá a repetir.
Un ángel marchoso pone
su cabeza en un cojín.
Otros de rubor cansado,
encendieron un candil.
Y cuando los cuatro primos
llegan a Benamejí,
voces de muerte cesaron
cerca del Guadalquivir.

ROMANCE DEL EMPLAZADO

¡Mi soledad sin descanso!
Ojos chicos de mi cuerpo
y grandes de mi caballo,
no se cierran por la noche
ni miran al otro lado,
donde se aleja tranquilo
un sueño de trece barcos.
Sino que, limpios y duros
escuderos desvelados,

coin which never will be repeated. A swaggering angel places his head on a cushion. Others with a wearied blush lighted an oil-lamp. And when the four cousins arrive at Benamejí, voices of death ceased near the Guadalquivir.

Ballad of the Accursed ★

My unquiet solitude! Small eyes of my body and big eyes of my horse never close at night nor look to the farther side, where quietly a dream of thirteen boats sails away. Instead, clear and sharp vigilant

---

★ Literally, a specific curse, summoning one to appear before God on a given day.

mis ojos miran un norte
de metales y peñascos
donde mi cuerpo sin venas
consulta naipes helados.

★

Los densos bueyes del agua
embisten a los muchachos
que se bañan en las lunas
de sus cuernos ondulados.
Y los martillos cantaban
sobre los yunques sonámbulos
el insomnio del jinete
y el insomnio del caballo.

★

El veinticinco de junio
le dijeron a el Amargo:
«Ya puedes cortar, si gustas,
las adelfas de tu patio.
Pinta una cruz en la puerta
y pon tu nombre debajo,
porque cicutas y ortigas

---

squires, my eyes look on a pole-star of metals and rugged rocks where my body empty of veins consults frozen playing cards.

The massive oxen of the water★ rush against youths bathing in the moons of their undulating horns. And over somnambular anvils, hammers sang the insomnia of the rider and the insomnia of the horse.

On June the twenty-fifth they told Amargo: 'You can now cut the oleanders in your patio if you wish. Paint a cross on your door and put your name underneath, because hemlocks and nettles will

---

★ Here Lorca takes from Andalusian folk-lore the expression '*un buey de agua*' (a water ox), signifying a slow but deep and powerful water-course, and transforms the image to suit his poetical context.

nacerán en tu costado,
y agujas de cal mojada
te morderán los zapatos.
Será de noche, en lo oscuro,
por los montes imantados,
donde los bueyes del agua
beben los juncos soñando.
Pide luces y campanas.
Aprende a cruzar las manos
y gusta los aires fríos
de metales y peñascos.
Porque dentro de dos meses
yacerás amortajado.»

★

Espadón de nebulosa
mueve en el aire Santiago.
Grave silencio, de espalda,
manaba el cielo combado.

★

El veinticinco de junio
abrió sus ojos Amargo,
y el veinticinco de agosto
se tendió para cerrarlos.

---

grow from your sides, and needles of moistened lime will bite your shoes. It will be at night, in the dark, through the magnetic hills, where the oxen of the water dreamily drink the rushes. Ask for lights and bells. Learn how to cross your hands, and relish the cold breezes of metals and rugged rocks. Because within two months you will lie in a shroud.'

St James waves a nebular sword in the air. Oppressive silence flowed from the back of the arched sky.

On the twenty-fifth of June Amargo opened his eyes, and on the twenty-fifth of August he lay down to close them. Men came down

Hombres bajaban la calle
para ver al emplazado,
que fijaba sobre el muro
su soledad con descanso.
Y la sábana impecable,
de duro acento romano,
daba equilibrio a la muerte
con las rectas de sus paños.

ROMANCE DE LA GUARDIA CIVIL ESPAÑOLA

Los caballos negros son.
Las herraduras son negras.
Sobre las capas relucen
manchas de tinta y de cera.
Tienen, por eso no lloran,
de plomo las calaveras.
Con el alma de charol
vienen por la carretera.
Jorobados y nocturnos,
por donde animan ordenan
silencios de goma oscura
y miedos de fina arena.
Pasan, si quieren pasar,

the street to see the accursed, whose solitude at rest was fixed on the wall. And the spotless sheet, of strong Roman lines, with the sharp corners of its panels gave death its equilibrium.

Ballad of the Spanish Civil Guard

The horses are black. Black are the horse-shoes. Ink and wax stains shine on their cloaks. They have skulls of lead, this is why they do not weep. With their patent-leather souls they come along the road. Hunchbacked and nocturnal, wherever they stir they command silences of dark rubber and fears of fine sand. They pass, if they wish

y ocultan en la cabeza
una vaga astronomía
de pistolas inconcretas.

      *

¡Oh ciudad de los gitanos!
En las esquinas, banderas.
La luna y la calabaza
con las guindas en conserva.
¡Oh ciudad de los gitanos!
¿Quién te vió y no te recuerda?
Ciudad de dolor y almizcle,
con las torres de canela.

      *

Cuando llegaba la noche,
noche que noche nochera,
los gitanos en sus fraguas
forjaban soles y flechas.
Un caballo malherido
llamaba a todas las puertas.
Gallos de vidrio cantaban
por Jerez de la Frontera.
El viento vuelve desnudo
la esquina de la sorpresa,

to pass, and they hide in their heads a vague astronomy of undefined pistols.

Oh, city of the gipsies! Flags on the street corners. The moon, and the pumpkin with the preserved cherries. Oh, city of the gipsies! Who that saw you would forget? City of sorrow and musk, and cinnamon-coloured towers.

When night drew close, night, deep night of nights, the gipsies in their forges shaped suns and arrows. A mortally wounded horse knocked at all the doors. Glass cocks sang in Jerez de la Frontera. The wind turns naked the corner of surprise, in the night, silver

en la noche platinoche,
noche que noche nochera.

★

La Virgen y San José
perdieron sus castañuelas,
y buscan a los gitanos
para ver si las encuentran.
La Virgen viene vestida
con un traje de alcaldesa,
de papel de chocolate
con los collares de almendras.
San José mueve los brazos
bajo una capa de seda.
Detrás va Pedro Domecq
con tres sultanes de Persia.
La media luna soñaba
un éxtasis de cigüeña.
Estandartes y faroles
invaden las azoteas.
Por los espejos sollozan
bailarinas sin caderas.
Agua y sombra, sombra y agua
por Jerez de la Frontera.

★

night, night, deep night of nights.

The Virgin and Saint Joseph lost their castanets, and they seek out the gipsies to see if they can find them. The Virgin comes dressed in a mayoress's gown of chocolate paper and with almond necklaces. Saint Joseph moves his arms under a silk cloak. Behind follow Pedro Domecq with three sultans of Persia. The half moon was dreaming the ecstasy of a stork. Banners and lanterns invade the flat roofs. In the mirrors wail hipless girl-dancers. Water and shadow, shadow and water at Jerez de la Frontera.

¡Oh ciudad de los gitanos!
En las esquinas, banderas.
Apaga tus verdes luces
que viene la benemérita.
¡Oh ciudad de los gitanos!
¿Quién te vió y no te recuerda?
Dejadla lejos del mar,
sin peines para sus crenchas.

★

Avanzan de dos en fondo
a la ciudad de la fiesta.
Un rumor de siemprevivas
invade las cartucheras.
Avanzan de dos en fondo.
Doble nocturno de tela.
El cielo, se les antoja
una vitrina de espuelas.

★

La ciudad, libre de miedo,
multiplicaba sus puertas.
Cuarenta guardias civiles
entran a saco por ellas.
Los relojes se pararon,
y el coñac de las botellas

Oh, city of the gipsies! Flags on the street corners. Put out your
green lights, the Civil Guard is coming. Oh, city of the gipsies! Who
that saw you would forget? Leave her away from the sea, with no
combs to part her hair.

They advance two abreast towards the festive city. A murmur of
immortelles invades the cartridge-belts. They advance two abreast.
Nocturnal duplication of cloth. They imagine the sky to be a show-
window of spurs.

The city, free from fear, multiplied its doors. Forty Civil Guards
go through them to plunder. The clocks stopped, and the brandy in

se disfrazó de noviembre
para no infundir sospechas.
Un vuelo de gritos largos
se levantó en las veletas.
Los sables cortan las brisas
que los cascos atropellan.
Por las calles de penumbra
huyen las gitanas viejas
con los caballos dormidos
y las orzas de monedas.
Por las calles empinadas
suben las capas siniestras,
dejando detrás fugaces
remolinos de tijeras.

En el portal de Belén
los gitanos se congregan.
San José, lleno de heridas,
amortaja a una doncella.
Tercos fusiles agudos
por toda la noche suenan.
La Virgen cura a los niños
con salivilla de estrella.
Pero la Guardia Civil
avanza sembrando hogueras,

the bottles disguised itself as November not to arouse suspicion. A
flight of sustained shrieks rose from the weathercocks. The sabres
cut the breezes trampled by the hooves. Along the darkened streets
old gipsy women fled, taking the sleeping horses and the crocks of
coins. Up though the steep street go the sinister cloaks, leaving in
their wake brief whirlpools of scissors.

At the Gate of Bethlehem the gipsies assembled. Saint Joseph,
covered with wounds, puts a shroud on a maiden. Sharp stubborn
rifles sputter all through the night. The Virgin heals children with
the spittle of stars. But the Civil Guard advance sowing fires, where

donde joven y desnuda
la imaginación se quema.
Rosa la de los Camborios
gime sentada en su puerta
con sus dos pechos cortados
puestos en una bandeja.
Y otras muchachas corrían
perseguidas por sus trenzas,
en un aire donde estallan
rosas de pólvora negra.
Cuando todos los tejados
eran surcos en la tierra,
el alba meció sus hombros
en largo perfil de piedra.

★

¡Oh ciudad de los gitanos!
La Guardia Civil se aleja
por un túnel de silencio
mientras las llamas te cercan.

¡Oh ciudad de los gitanos!
¿Quién te vió y no te recuerda?
Que te busquen en mi frente.
Juego de luna y arena.

tender and naked the imagination burns out. Rosa of the Camborios moans sitting on her door-step, with both her cut-off breasts lying on a platter. While other girls run pursued by their plaits through air where roses of black gunpowder burst. When all the roofs were furrows in the earth, daybreak rocked its shoulders in a long profile of stone.

Oh, city of the gipsies! The Civil Guard move away through a tunnel of silence while flames encircle you.

Oh, city of the gipsies! Who that saw you would forget? On my forehead you will be found. Interplay of moon and sand.

THAMAR Y AMNÓN

La luna gira en el cielo
sobre las tierras sin agua
mientras el verano siembra
rumores de tigre y llama.
Por encima de los techos
nervios de metal sonaban.
Aire rizado venía
con los balidos de lana.
La tierra se ofrece llena
de heridas cicatrizadas,
o estremecida de agudos
cauterios de luces blancas.

★

Thamar estaba soñando
pájaros en su garganta,
al son de panderos fríos
y cítaras enlunadas.
Su desnudo en el alero,
agudo norte de palma,
pide copos a su vientre
y granizo a sus espaldas.
Thamar estaba cantando
desnuda por la terraza.

Thamar and Amnon

The moon revolves in the sky above waterless lands while summer scatters murmurs of tiger and flame. Over the roofs rang nerves of metal. Frizzled air drifted with the woolly bleatings. The earth presents itself covered with scars, or shuddering with the intense searing of white lights.

Thamar was dreaming of birds in her throat, to the sound of cool tambourines and moon-drenched citherns. Her naked body on the eaves, delicate palm pointer, asks for snowflakes on her belly and hail on her shoulders. Thamar was singing naked on the terrace. Around

Alrededor de sus pies,
cinco palomas heladas.
Amnón, delgado y concreto,
en la torre la miraba,
llenas las ingles de espuma
y oscilaciones la barba.
Su desnudo iluminado
se tendía en la terraza,
con un rumor entre dientes
de flecha recién clavada.
Amnón estaba mirando
la luna redonda y baja,
y vió en la luna los pechos
durísimos de su hermana.

⋆

Amnón a las tres y media
se tendió sobre la cama.
Toda la alcoba sufría
con sus ojos llenos de alas.
La luz maciza sepulta
pueblos en la arena parda,
o descubre transitorio
coral de rosas y dalias.
Linfa de pozo oprimida
brota silencio en las jarras.

her feet, five frozen pigeons. Amnon, slender and concrete, gazed at
her from the tower, his groins foaming and his beard quivering. Her
radiant nakedness stretched out on the terrace, with the murmur of
a newly struck arrow between her teeth. Amnon gazed at the round
and low moon, and in the moon he saw his sister's very firm breasts.

At half past three Amnon stretched himself on his bed. The
entire chamber suffered with the fluttering of his eyes. The solid
light buries villages in the brown sand, or discovers brief coral of
roses and dahlias. Oppressed water from the well blossoms into

En el musgo de los troncos
la cobra tendida canta.
Amnón gime por la tela
fresquísima de la cama.
Yedra del escalofrío
cubre su carne quemada.
Thamar entró silenciosa
en la alcoba silenciada,
color de vena y Danubio,
turbia de huellas lejanas.
«Thamar, bórrame los ojos
con tu fija madrugada.
Mis hilos de sangre tejen
volantes sobre tu falda.»
«Déjame tranquila, hermano.
Son tus besos en mi espalda
avispas y vientecillos
en doble enjambre de flautas.»
«Thamar, en tus pechos altos
hay dos peces que me llaman,
y en las yemas de tus dedos
rumor de rosa encerrada.»

★

silence in the jars. In the moss of tree-stems the stretched-out cobra sings. Amnon groans between the cold sheets of his bed. The ivy of a shiver creeps over his burnt flesh. Thamar, colour of vein and Danube, troubled with distant traces, entered silently into the silenced chamber. 'Thamar, blot out my eyes with your fixed dawn. The threads of my blood weave frills over your lap.' 'Leave me in peace, brother. On my shoulder your kisses are wasps and light winds in a double swarm of flutes.' 'Thamar, in your high breasts there are two fishes calling me, and in the tips of your fingers there are murmurs of unopened rose.'

Los cien caballos del rey
en el patio relinchaban.
Sol en cubos resistía
la delgadez de la parra.
Ya la coge del cabello,
ya la camisa le rasga.
Corales tibios dibujan
arroyos en rubio mapa.

★

¡Oh, qué gritos se sentían
por encima de las casas!
Qué espesura de puñales
y túnicas desgarradas.
Por las escaleras tristes
esclavos suben y bajan.
Émbolos y muslos juegan
bajo las nubes paradas.
Alrededor de Thamar
gritan vírgenes gitanas
y otras recogen las gotas
de su flor martirizada.
Paños blancos enrojecen
en las alcobas cerradas.
Rumores de tibia aurora
pámpanos y peces cambian.

The hundred horses of the king neighed in the courtyard. The slenderness of the vine resisted a downpour of sun. Now he grasps her by the hair, now he tears her shift. Tepid corals draw rivulets on a fair map.

Oh, what shrieks were heard above the houses! What thickness of daggers and ripped-up tunics. Slaves go up and down the gloomy stairways. Pistons and thighs play under still clouds. Around Thamar gipsy virgins scream, and others gather the drops of her martyrized flower. White fabrics redden in the locked chambers. Murmurs of faint daybreak transform vine-tendrils and fishes.

★

Violador enfurecido,
Amnón huye con su jaca.
Negros le dirigen flechas
en los muros y atalayas.
Y cuando los cuatro cascos
eran cuatro resonancias,
David con unas tijeras
cortó las cuerdas del arpa.

EL REY DE HARLEM

CON una cuchara
arrancaba los ojos a los cocodrilos
y golpeaba el trasero de los monos.
Con una cuchara.

Fuego de siempre dormía en los pedernales
y los escarabajos borrachos de anís
olvidaban el musgo de las aldeas.

Aquel viejo cubierto de setas
iba al sitio donde lloraban los negros

Infuriated violator, Amnon flees on his mare. Negroes aim arrows at him from ramparts and towers. And when the four hooves were four echoes, David, with a pair of scissors, cut the strings of the harp.

The King of Harlem

WITH a spoon he scooped out the eyes of crocodiles and whacked monkeys on their bottoms. With a spoon.

Eternal fire lay dormant in flint-stones, and cockroaches drunken with *anís* were forgetting the moss of the villages.

That old man, covered with mushrooms, was going to the place

mientras crujía la cuchara del rey
y llegaban los tanques de agua podrida.

Las rosas huían por los filos
de las últimas curvas del aire,
y en los montones de azafrán
los niños machacaban pequeñas ardillas
con un rubor de frenesí manchado.

Es preciso cruzar los puentes
y llegar al rubor negro
para que el perfume de pulmón
nos golpee las sienes con su vestido
de caliente piña.

Es preciso matar al rubio vendedor de aguardiente,
a todos los amigos de manzana y de la arena,
y es necesario dar con los puños cerrados
a las pequeñas judías que tiemblan llenas de burbujas,
para que el rey de Harlem cante con su muchedumbre,
para que los cocodrilos duerman en largas filas
bajo el amianto de la luna,
y para que nadie dude de la infinita belleza

where the Negroes wept, while the king's spoon crackled, and the tanks of putrid water arrived.

Roses escaped along the edges of the last curves of the air, and in heaps of saffron children crushed little squirrels with a flush of stained frenzy.

One must go across the bridges and arrive at the Negro blush in order to feel the lung's scent beating against our temples with its suit of warm pineapple.

One must kill the blond seller of brandy, and all the friends of the apple and the sand, and one must beat with closed fists the little haricot beans which tremble full of bubbles, so that the King of Harlem may sing with his multitude, so that the crocodiles may sleep in long rows under the asbestos of the moon, and so that nobody

de los plumeros, los ralladores, los cobres y las cacerolas
de las cocinas.

¡Ay, Harlem! ¡Ay, Harlem! ¡Ay, Harlem!
No hay angustia comparable a tus rojos oprimidos,
a tu sangre estremecida dentro del eclipse oscuro,
a tu violencia granate sordomuda en la penumbra,
a tu gran rey prisionero, con un traje de conserje.

★

Tenía la noche una hendidura y quietas salamandras de
marfil.
Las muchachas americanas
llevaban niños y monedas en el vientre
y los muchachos se desmayaban en la cruz del desperezo.

Ellos son.
Ellos son los que beben el whisky de plata junto a los
volcanes
y tragan pedacitos de corazón por las heladas montañas
del oso.

may doubt the infinite beauty of feather-dusters, graters, coppers,
and kitchen saucepans.

Ah, Harlem! Ah, Harlem! Ah, Harlem! There is no anguish to
compare with your oppressed reds, or with the shudder of your
blood within the dark eclipse, or with your garnet-coloured violence
deaf and dumb in the half-light, or with your great imprisoned king
in a commissionaire's uniform.

The night was cleft and held quiet ivory salamanders. American
girls carried children and coins in their bellies, and youths fainted on
the cross of the slow awakening.

They are. They are the ones that drink silver whisky by the vol-
canoes and swallow fragments of heart on the frozen mountains of
the bear.

Aquella noche el rey de Harlem con una durísima cuchara
arrancaba los ojos a los cocodrilos
y golpeaba el trasero de los monos.
Con una cuchara.
Los negros lloraban confundidos
entre paraguas y soles de oro,
los mulatos estiraban gomas, ansiosos de llegar al torso
      blanco,
y el viento empañaba espejos
y quebraba las venas de los bailarines.

Negros, Negros, Negros, Negros.

La sangre no tiene puertas en vuestra noche boca arriba.
No hay rubor. Sangre furiosa por debajo de las pieles,
viva en la espina del puñal y en el pecho de los paisajes,
bajo las pinzas y las retamas de la celeste luna de cáncer.

Sangre que busca por mil caminos muertes enharinadas
      y ceniza de nardo,
cielos yertos, en declive, donde las colonias de planetas
rueden por las playas con los objetos abandonados.

On that night the King of Harlem with a very hard spoon
scooped out the eyes of crocodiles and whacked the monkeys on
their bottoms. With a spoon. Negroes wept perplexed among
umbrellas and golden suns, mulattos stretched gum, anxious to reach
the white torso, and the wind clouded mirrors and crushed the veins
of dancers.
    Negroes, Negroes, Negroes, Negroes.
    Blood has no doors in your upturned night. There is no flush of
blood. Blood raging under the skins, living in the thorn of the dag-
ger and in the heart of landscapes, under the pincers and genistas of
the celestial moon of cancer.
    Blood that searches along a thousand ways flour-covered deaths
and tuberose ash, and rigid slanting skies, where clusters of planets
may roll about the beaches together with forsaken objects.

Sangre que mira lenta con el rabo del ojo,
hecha de espartos exprimidos, néctares de subterráneos.
Sangre que oxida el alisio descuidado en una huella
y disuelve a las mariposas en los cristales de la ventana.

Es la sangre que viene, que vendrá
por los tejados y azoteas, por todas partes,
para quemar la clorofilia de las mujeres rubias,
para gemir al pie de las camas ante el insomnio de los
      lavabos
y estrellarse en una aurora de tabaco y bajo amarillo.

Hay que huir,
huir por las esquinas y encerrarse en los últimos pisos,
porque el tuétano del bosque penetrará por las rendijas
para dejar en vuestra carne una leve huella de eclipse
y una falsa tristeza de guante desteñido y rosa química.

      *

Es por el silencio sapientísimo
cuando los camareros y los cocineros y los que limpian
      con la lengua

Blood that looks askance unhurried, composed of pressed-out
esparto, nectar of basements. Blood oxidizing the trade-wind listless
in a footprint, and dissolving moths on window-panes.

It is the blood that comes, that will come along roof-tops, and
terraces, from all sides, to burn the chlorophyll of blonde women, to
moan at the foot of beds face to face with the insomnia of basins,
and to crash against a tobacco and dull yellow daybreak.

One must escape, escape round the corners and lock oneself in
the top stories, because the pith of the forest will penetrate the
cracks to leave in your flesh a soft print of eclipse and a false sadness
of faded glove and chemical rose.

It is in the wisest silence that waiters and cooks and those who
with their tongues lick the wounds of millionaires, look for the king

las heridas de los millonarios
buscan al rey por las calles o en los ángulos del salitre.

Un viento sur de madera, oblicuo en el negro fango,
escupe a las barcas rotas y se clava puntillas en los
      hombros;
un viento sur que lleva
colmillos, girasoles, alfabetos
y una pila de Volta con avispas ahogadas.

El olvido estaba expresado por tres gotas de tinta sobre el
      monóculo,
el amor por un solo rostro invisible a flor de piedra.
Médulas y corolas componían sobre las nubes
un desierto de tallos sin una sola rosa.

      ★

A la izquierda, a la derecha, por el sur y por el norte,
se levanta el muro impasible
para el topo, la aguja del agua.
No busquéis, negros, su grieta
para hallar la máscara infinita.
Buscad el gran sol del centro

in the streets or on the sharp corners of saltpetre.
    A woody south wind, slanting in the black mud, spits at the
wrecked boats and pierces its shoulders with tacks; a south wind
carrying tusks, sunflowers, alphabets, and an electric battery with
wasps drowned in it.
    Oblivion revealed itself by three drops of ink on the monocle,
and love by a single invisible face on the stone's surface. Pith and
corollas formed on the clouds a desert of stems without a single
rose.
    To the left, to the right, Southwards and Northwards, there rises
a wall insensible to the mole or the needle of water. Do not seek,
Negroes, for a cleavage in it to find the infinite mask. Yourselves
turned into a buzzing cone, search for the great sun of the centre.

hechos una piña zumbadora.
El sol que se desliza por los bosques
seguro de no encontrar una ninfa,
el sol que destruye números y no ha cruzado nunca un
    sueño,
el tatuado sol que baja por el río
y muge seguido de caimanes.

Negros, Negros, Negros, Negros.

Jamás sierpe, ni cebra, ni mula
palidecieron al morir.
El leñador no sabe cuándo expiran
los clamorosos árboles que corta.
Aguardad bajo la sombra vegetal de vuestro rey
a que cicutas y cardos y ortigas turben postreras azoteas.

Entonces, negros, entonces, entonces,
podréis besar con frenesí las ruedas de las bicicletas,
poner parejas de microscopios en las cuevas de las ardillas
y danzar al fin, sin duda, mientras las flores erizadas
asesinan a nuestro Moisés casi en los juncos del cielo.

The sun that glides through the woods certain of not finding a
nymph, the sun that destroys numbers and has never penetrated a
dream, the tattooed sun flowing down the river, and bellowing with
alligators on its trail.

Negroes, Negroes, Negroes, Negroes.

Never did snake, nor zebra, nor mule, grow pale at death. The
woodcutter does not know when the screeching trees which he fells
expire. Wait beneath the vegetable shadow of your king until hem-
locks and thistles and stinging-nettles disturb the most remote roof-
terraces.

Then, Negroes, then, then, you will be able to kiss frantically the
wheels of bicycles, to put pairs of microscopes in squirrels' nests, and
to dance at last, assured, while the bristling flowers murder our
Moses close to the reeds of heaven.

¡Ay, Harlem, disfrazada!
¡Ay, Harlem, amenazada por un gentío de trajes sin
   cabeza!
Me llega tu rumor,
me llega tu rumor atravesando troncos y ascensores,
a través de láminas grises,
donde flotan tus automóviles cubiertos de dientes,
a través de los caballos muertos y los crímenes
   diminutos,
a través de tu gran rey desesperado
cuyas barbas llegan al mar.

LA AURORA

La aurora de Nueva York tiene
cuatro columnas de cieno
y un huracán de negras palomas
que chapotean las aguas podridas.

La aurora de Nueva York gime
por las inmensas escaleras
buscando entre las aristas
nardos de angustia dibujada.

Ah, masqueraded Harlem! Ah, Harlem threatened by a multitude of headless suits! Your murmur reaches me, your murmur reaches me through tree-trunks and lifts, through grey metal plates, where your automobiles covered with teeth float, through dead horses and petty crimes, through your great forlorn king whose beard reaches the sea.

Daybreak

New York's daybreak has four columns of mire and a hurricane of black doves paddling in putrescent waters.

New York's daybreak moans along the immense stairways, seeking between ledges tuberoses of delineated anguish.

La aurora llega y nadie la recibe en su boca
porque allí no hay mañana ni esperanza posible.
A veces las monedas en enjambres furiosos
taladran y devoran abandonados niños.

Los primeros que salen comprenden con sus huesos
que no habrá paraíso ni amores deshojados;
saben que van al cieno de números y leyes,
a los juegos sin arte, a sudores sin fruto.

La luz es sepultada por cadenas y ruidos
en impúdico reto de ciencia sin raíces.
Por los barrios hay gentes que vacilan insomnes
como recién salidas de un naufragio de sangre.

POEMA DOBLE DEL LAGO EDEN

Era mi voz antigua
ignorante de los densos jugos amargos.
La adivino lamiendo mis pies
bajo los frágiles helechos mojados.

Daybreak comes and no one receives it in the mouth, for no morning nor hope is possible there. At times, coins in furious swarms perforate and devour abandoned children.

The first to go out understand in their bones that there will be no paradise nor natural love; they know they are going to the mire of figures and laws, to artless games, to fruitless sweat.

Chains and noises bury the light in a shameless challenge of rootless science. Along the suburbs sleepless crowds stagger, as though freshly delivered from a shipwreck of blood.

Double Poem of Lake Eden

My ancient voice was unaware of the dense bitter juices. I divine it licking my feet under the drenched and fragile ferns.

¡Ay voz antigua de mi amor,
ay voz de mi verdad,
ay voz de mi abierto costado,
cuando todas las rosas manaban de mi lengua
y el césped no conocía la impasible dentadura del
    caballo!

Estás aquí bebiendo mi sangre,
bebiendo mi humor de niño pesado,
mientras mis ojos se quiebran en el viento
con el aluminio y las voces de los borrachos.

Déjame pasar la puerta
donde Eva come hormigas
y Adán fecunda peces deslumbrados.
Déjame pasar hombrecillo de los cuernos
al bosque de los desperezos
y los alegrísimos saltos.

Yo sé el uso más secreto
que tiene un viejo alfiler oxidado
y sé del horror de unos ojos despiertos
sobre la superficie concreta del plato.

Ah, ancient voice of my love, ah, voice of my reality, ah, voice of
my opened side, when every rose sprang from my tongue, and the
grass knew not the horse's insensible teeth!

You are here drinking my blood, drinking my tiresome child's
temper, while in the wind my eyes break against aluminium and
voices of drunkards.

Let me pass though the door where Eve eats ants, and Adam
fertilizes dazzled fishes. Horned dwarf, let me pass though to the
wood of yawnings and stretchings, and of exhilarating jumps.

I know the most secret use of an old rusty pin, and I know the
horror of wide-open eyes on the tangible surface of the dish.

Pero no quiero mundo ni sueño, voz divina,
quiero mi libertad, mi amor humano
en el rincón más oscuro de la brisa que nadie quiera.
¡Mi amor humano!

Esos perros marinos se persiguen
y el viento acecha troncos descuidados.
¡Oh voz antigua, quema con tu lengua
esta voz de hojalata y de talco!

Quiero llorar porque me da la gana
como lloran los niños del último banco,
porque yo no soy un hombre, ni un poeta, ni una hoja,
pero sí un pulso herido que sonda las cosas del otro lado.

Quiero llorar diciendo mi nombre,
rosa, niño y abeto a la orilla de este lago,
para decir mi verdad de hombre de sangre
matando en mí la burla y la sugestión del vocablo.

No, no, yo no pregunto, yo deseo,
voz mía libertada que me lames las manos.

But I want not world or dream, divine voice, I want my freedom, my human love in the most obscure corner of a breeze wanted by no one. My human love!

Those sea-dogs pursue each other, and the wind waylays unsuspecting tree-trunks. Oh, ancient voice, burn with your tongue this voice of tin and talcum!

I want to cry because it so pleases me, as children in the last bench do cry, because I am not a man, nor a poet, nor a leaf; I am a wounded pulse probing what lies on the other side.

I want to weep calling out my name, rose, child, and fir-tree on this lake's shore, to pronounce my truth of full-blooded man, stifling in me the sneer and the suggestion of the word.

No, no, I do not ask; I desire, freed voice of mine, that you should

En el laberinto de biombos es mi desnudo el que recibe
la luna de castigo y el reloj encenizado.

Así hablaba yo.
Así hablaba yo cuando Saturno detuvo los trenes
y la bruma y el Sueño y la Muerte me estaban
        buscando.
Me estaban buscando
allí donde mugen las vacas que tienen patitas de paje
y allí donde flota mi cuerpo entre los equilibrios
        contrarios.

CIELO VIVO

Yo no podré quejarme
si no encontré lo que buscaba.
Cerca de las piedras sin jugo y los insectos vacíos
no veré el duelo del sol con las criaturas en carne viva.

Pero me iré al primer paisaje
de choques, líquidos y rumores
que trasmina a niño recién nacido

lick my hands. In the labyrinth of screens it is my nakedness that
receives the looking-glass of punishment and the cindery clock.

Thus I spoke. Thus I spoke when Saturn stopped the trains, and
fog and Dream and Death were all seeking me. They were seeking
me where the lowing cows of page-like feet are, and where coun-
terpoised my body floats.

Living Heaven

I SHALL not complain if I failed to find what I was seeking. Near
the juiceless stones and the empty insects I shall not see the duel of
the sun with raw-flesh creatures.

But I shall go to the first landscape of collisions, liquids, and mur-
murs pervading new-born child, and where every outer surface is

y donde toda superficie es evitada,
para entender que lo que busco tendrá su blanco de
    alegría
cuando yo vuele mezclado con el amor y las arenas.

Allí no llega la escarcha de los ojos apagados
ni el mugido del árbol asesinado por la oruga.
Allí todas las formas guardan entrelazadas
una sola expresión frenética de avance.

No puedes avanzar por los enjambres de corolas
porque el aire disuelve tus dientes de azúcar,
ni puedes acariciar la fugaz hoja del helecho
sin sentir el asombro definitivo del marfil.

Allí bajo las raíces y en la médula del aire
se comprende la verdad de las cosas equivocadas,
el nadador de níquel que acecha la onda más fina
y el rebaño de vacas nocturnas con rojas patitas de mujer.

Yo no podré quejarme
si no encontré lo que buscaba;
pero me iré al primer paisaje de humedades y latidos

avoided, in order to understand that what I seek will have its target
of joy when mingled with love and sand I move through the air.

    Frost of darkened eyes does not reach there, nor the groan of the
tree murdered by the caterpillar. There, every shape holds entwined
a single delirious forward expression.

    You cannot advance though the swarms of corollas because the
air dissolves your teeth of sugar, nor can you caress the fleeting fern-
leaf without feeling the final astonishment of ivory.

    There, under the roots, and in the air's marrow we shall grasp the
truth of what is not right, of the nickel swimmer lying in wait for
the finest wave, and of the herd of nocturnal cows with small femi-
nine red feet.

    I shall not complain if I failed to find what I was seeking; but I
shall go to the first landscape of dampness and heart-beats in order

para entender que lo que busco tendrá su blanco de
    alegría
cuando yo vuele mezclado con el amor y las arenas.

Vuelo fresco de siempre sobre lechos vacíos,
sobre grupos de brisas y barcos encallados.
Tropiezo vacilante por la dura eternidad fija
y amor al fin sin alba. Amor. ¡Amor visible!

ODA A WALT WHITMAN

Por el East River y el Bronx
los muchachos cantaban enseñando sus cinturas,
con la rueda, el aceite, el cuero y el martillo.
Noventa mil mineros sacaban la plata de las rocas
y los niños dibujaban escaleras y perspectivas.

Pero ninguno se dormía,
ninguno quería ser el río,
ninguno amaba las hojas grandes,
ninguno la lengua azul de la playa.

to understand that what I seek will reach its target of joy when mingled with love and sand I move though the air.

With my innate freshness I soar over empty river-beds, over clustered breezes and stranded boats. Uncertain, I stumble in the hard, constant eternity, and love eventually without daybreak. Love. Open love!

Ode to Walt Whitman

ALONG East River and the Bronx youths were singing, stripped to the waist, with the wheel, the oil, the leather, and the hammer. Ninety thousand miners extracted silver from rocks, and children drew scales and perspectives.

But none would sleep, none wanted to be the river, none cared for the great leaves, none for the blue tongue of the beach.

Por el East River y el Queensborough
los muchachos luchaban con la industria,
y los judíos vendían al fauno del río
la rosa de la circuncisión
y el cielo desembocaba por los puentes y los tejados
manadas de bisontes empujadas por el viento.

Pero ninguno se detenía,
ninguno quería ser nube,
ninguno buscaba los helechos
ni la rueda amarilla del tamboril.

Cuando la luna salga
las poleas rodarán para turbar el cielo;
un límite de agujas cercará la memoria
y los ataúdes se llevarán a los que no trabajan.

Nueva York de cieno,
Nueva York de alambres y de muerte.
¿Qué ángel llevas oculto en la mejilla?
¿Qué voz perfecta dirá las verdades del trigo?
¿Quién el sueño terrible de tus anémonas manchadas?

Along East River and Queensborough youths were fighting with Industry, and the Jews were selling the rose of circumcision to the faun of the river, and the sky through bridges and roofs poured herds of bison driven by the wind.

But none would pause, none wanted to be a cloud, none would seek ferns nor the yellow hoop of the tambourine.

At moonrise pulleys will turn and thus tumble down* the sky; a boundary of needles will encircle the memory, and coffins will carry away those who do not work.

New York of slime, New York of wires and death. What angel do you hold concealed in your cheek? What faultless voice will speak the truths of the wheat? Who, the terrible dream of your stained anemones?

---

* Translating *tumbar*; the modern reading *turbar* means 'disturb'. [Ed.]

Ni un solo momento, viejo hermoso Walt Whitman,
he dejado de ver tu barba llena de mariposas,
ni tus hombros de pana gastados por la luna,
ni tus muslos de Apolo virginal,
ni tu voz como una columna de ceniza;
anciano hermoso como la niebla
que gemías igual que un pájaro
con el sexo atravesado por una aguja,
enemigo del sátiro,
enemigo de la vid
y amante de los cuerpos bajo la burda tela.

Ni un solo momento, hermosura viril
que en montes de carbón, anuncios y ferrocarriles,
soñabas ser un río y dormir como un río
con aquel camarada que pondría en tu pecho
un pequeño dolor de ignorante leopardo.

Ni un solo momento, Adán de sangre, macho,
hombre solo en el mar, viejo hermoso Walt Whitman,
porque por las azoteas,
agrupados en los bares,
saliendo en racimos de las alcantarillas,

Not for one moment, beautiful aged Walt Whitman, have I failed to see your beard full of butterflies, nor your corduroy shoulders worn thin by the moon, nor your thighs of virginal Apollo, nor your voice like a pillar of ashes; ancient and beautiful as the mist, you moaned like a bird with the sex transfixed by a needle, enemy of the satyr, enemy of the vine, and lover of bodies under the rough cloth. Not for one moment, virile beauty, who in mountains of coal, posters, and railways, dreamed of being a river and sleeping like a river with that comrade who would place in your breast the small pain of an ignorant leopard. Not for one moment, Adam of blood, male, lone man in the sea, beautiful aged Walt Whitman, because in terraces, crowding in bars, pouring out of sewers in bunches, trembling between the legs of

temblando entre las piernas de los chauffeurs
o girando en las plataformas del ajenjo,
los maricas, Walt Whitman, te soñaban.

¡También ése! ¡También! Y se despeñan
sobre tu barba luminosa y casta,
rubios del norte, negros de la arena,
muchedumbres de gritos y ademanes,
como gatos y como las serpientes,
los maricas, Walt Whitman, los maricas
turbios de lágrimas, carne para fusta,
bota o mordisco de los domadores.

¡También ése! ¡También! Dedos teñidos
apuntan a la orilla de tu sueño
cuando el amigo come tu manzana
con un leve sabor de gasolina
y el sol canta por los ombligos
de los muchachos que juegan bajo los puentes.

Pero tú no buscabas los ojos arañados,
ni el pantano oscurísimo donde sumergen a los niños,
ni la saliva helada,

chauffeurs or revolving on the platforms of absinth, the pansies, Walt
Whitman, dreamed of you.

This one also! Also! And they plunge on your chaste and resplen-
dent beard, Northern blonds, Negroes from the sands, shouting and
gesticulating multitudes, like cats or like snakes, the pansies, Walt
Whitman, the pansies, disordered with tears, flesh for the whip, boot,
or bite of subduers.

This one also! Also! Stained fingers point to the edge of your
dream while the friend eats your apple tasting faintly of petrol, and
the sun sings around the navels of youths playing under bridges.

But you were not seeking the scratched eyes, or the pitch-dark
swamp where children are submerged, or the frozen saliva, or the

ni las curvas heridas como panza de sapo
que llevan los maricas en coches y terrazas
mientras la luna los azota por las esquinas del terror.

Tú buscabas un desnudo que fuera como un río,
toro y sueño que junte la rueda con el alga,
padre de tu agonía, camelia de tu muerte,
y gimiera en las llamas de tu ecuador oculto.

Porque es justo que el hombre no busque su deleite
en la selva de sangre de la mañana próxima.
El cielo tiene playas donde evitar la vida
y hay cuerpos que no deben repetirse en la aurora.

Agonía, agonía, sueño, fermento y sueño.
Éste es el mundo, amigo, agonía, agonía.
Los muertos se descomponen bajo el reloj de las
    ciudades,
la guerra pasa llorando con un millón de ratas grises,
los ricos dan a sus queridas
pequeños moribundos iluminados,
y la vida no es noble, ni buena, ni sagrada.

curved wounds like toad's bellies which pansies carry in cars and
terraces while the moon whips them at the corners of fear.
    You sought a nakedness like a river. Bull and dream that would
join the wheel to the seaweed, father of your agony, camellia of your
death, and would moan in the flames of your hidden Equator.
    Because it is just that man seeks not his delight in the jungle of
blood of the approaching morning. Heaven has shores where life
can be avoided, and certain bodies should not be repeated at day-
break.
    Agony, agony, dream, ferment and dream. Such is the world, my
friend, agony, agony. Corpses are decomposing under the docks of
cities; war passes with a million grey rats weeping, the rich give to
their mistresses small illuminated moribund, and life is not noble,
nor good, nor sacred.

Puede el hombre, si quiere, conducir su deseo
por vena de coral o celeste desnudo.
Mañana los amores serán rocas y el Tiempo
una brisa que viene dormida por las ramas.

Por eso no levanto mi voz, viejo Walt Whitman,
contra el niño que escribe
nombre de niña en su almohada,
ni contra el muchacho que se viste de novia
en la oscuridad del ropero,
ni contra los solitarios de los casinos
que beben con asco el agua de la prostitución,
ni contra los hombres de mirada verde
que aman al hombre y queman sus labios en silencio.
Pero sí contra vosotros, maricas de las ciudades,
de carne tumefacta y pensamiento inmundo,
madres de lodo, arpías, enemigos sin sueño
del Amor que reparte coronas de alegría.

Contra vosotros siempre, que dais a los muchachos
gotas de sucia muerte con amargo veneno.
Contra vosotros siempre,
Faeries de Norteamérica,

Man can, if he wishes, lead his desire through vein of coral or
celestial nude. Gallantries will turn tomorrow into rocks, and Time
will be a breeze which comes asleep in the branches.

That is why I do not raise my voice, aged Walt Whitman, against
the little boy writing on his pillow a girl's name, nor against the
youth who puts on a bride's dress in the darkness of the wardrobe,
nor against solitary men in clubs who drink with nausea the water
of prostitution, nor against men of green glance who love man and
burn their lips in silence. But against you, yes, pansies of the cities,
with swollen flesh and unclean mind, dregs of mud, harpies, sleep-
less enemies of the Love that gives away garlands of joy.

Against you always, you who with bitter poison give youths
drops of soiled death. Against you always, *Fairies* of North America,

Pájaros de la Habana,
Jotos de Méjico,
Sarasas de Cádiz,
Apios de Sevilla,
Cancos de Madrid,
Floras de Alicante,
Adelaidas de Portugal.

¡Maricas de todo el mundo, asesinos de palomas!
Esclavos de la mujer, perras de sus tocadores,
abiertos en las plazas con fiebre de abanico
o emboscados en yertos paisajes de cicuta.

¡No haya cuartel! La muerte
mana de vuestros ojos
y agrupa flores grises en la orilla del cieno.
¡No haya cuartel! ¡Alerta!
Que los confundidos, los puros,
los clásicos, los señalados, los suplicantes
os cierren las puertas de la bacanal.

Y tú, bello Walt Whitman, duerme a orillas del Hudson
con la barba hacia el polo y las manos abiertas.

Pájaros of Havana, *Jotos* of Mexico, *Sarasas* of Cadiz, *Apios* of Seville,
Cancos of Madrid, *Floras* of Alicante, *Adelaidas* of Portugal.

Pansies of the world, murderers of doves! Women's slaves, bitch-
es of their boudoirs, spread in public squares with the fever of a fan
or ambushed in frigid landscapes of hemlock.

Let there be no quarter! Death flows from your eyes and heaps
grey flowers on the shores of the slime. Let there be no quarter!
Look out! Let the perplexed, the pure, the traditional, the noted, the
supplicants, close against you the gates of the Bacchanalia.

And you, beautiful Walt Whitman, sleep on the banks of the
Hudson, with your beard towards the pole and your hands open.

Arcilla blanda o nieve, tu lengua está llamando
camaradas que velen tu gacela sin cuerpo.

Duerme, no queda nada.
Una danza de muros agita las praderas
y América se anega de máquinas y llanto.
Quiero que el aire fuerte de la noche más honda
quite flores y letras del arco donde duermes
y un niño negro anuncie a los blancos del oro
la llegada del reino de la espiga.

PEQUEÑO POEMA INFINITO

Equivocar el camino
es llegar a la nieve
y llegar a la nieve
es pacer durante veinte siglos las hierbas de los
        cementerios.

Equivocar el camino
es llegar a la mujer,
la mujer que no teme la luz,

Bland clay or snow, your tongue calls out for comrades to keep watch on your disembodied gazelle.

Sleep, nothing remains. A dance of walls shakes the meadows, and America drowns itself in a flood of machines and tears. I want the strong wind of the deepest night to remove flowers and words from the vault where you lie asleep, and a black boy announcing to the gold-minded whites the arrival of the reign of the ear of corn.

Little Infinite Poem

To mistake the path is to reach the snow, and to reach the snow is to graze for twenty centuries on the grass of cemeteries.

To mistake the path is to reach woman, woman fearless of light,

la mujer que mata dos gallos en un segundo,
la luz que no teme a los gallos
y los gallos que no saben cantar sobre la nieve.

Pero si la nieve se equivoca de corazón
puede llegar el viento Austro
y como el aire no hace caso de los gemidos
tendremos que pacer otra vez las hierbas de los
    cementerios.

Yo vi dos dolorosas espigas de cera
que enterraban un paisaje de volcanes
y vi dos niños locos que empujaban llorando las
    pupilas de un asesino.

Pero el dos no ha sido nunca un número
porque es una angustia y su sombra,
porque es la guitarra donde el amor se desespera,
porque es la demostración de otro infinito que no es
    suyo
y es las murallas del muerto
y el castigo de la nueva resurrección sin finales.

woman killing two cockerels in one second, light fearless of cock-
erels, and cockerels unable to crow on the snow.

But should the snow mistake a heart, the Southern wind may
come, and since the air pays no heed to groans, we shall have to
graze again on the grass of cemeteries.

I saw two mournful spikes of wax burying a landscape of volca-
noes, and I saw two mad children, in tears, pushing the eye-balls of
a murderer.

But two was never a number because it is agony and its shadow,
because it is the guitar where love frets, because it is the proof of
another infinite not its own, and it is the ramparts of a corpse and
the punishment of the new resurrection without end. The dead hate

Los muertos odian el número dos
pero el número dos adormece a las mujeres
y como la mujer teme la luz
la luz tiembla delante de los gallos
y los gallos sólo saben volar sobre la nieve
tendremos que pacer sin descanso las hierbas de los
    cementerios.

NANA

SUEGRA: NANA, niño, nana
del caballo grande
que no quiso el agua.
El agua era negra
dentro de las ramas.
Cuando llega al puente
se detiene y canta.
¿Quién dirá, mi niño,
lo que tiene el agua,
con su larga cola
por su verde sala?

MUJER (*bajo*): Duérmete, clavel,
que el caballo no quiere beber.

number two, but number two lulls women to sleep, and since
woman fears light, and light shivers in front of cockerels, and only
cockerels know how to fly above the snow, we shall have to graze
for ever on the grass of cemeteries.

Lullaby

MOTHER-IN-LAW: Lullaby, child, lullaby of the big horse who
would not drink water. The water was black within the branches.
When it reaches the bridge it halts and sings. Who will say, my child,
what the water feels, trailing its tail in its green parlour?

    WOMAN (*softly*): Go to sleep, carnation, the horse will not drink.

| SUEGRA: | Duérmete, rosal,
que el caballo se pone a llorar.
Las patas heridas,
las crines heladas,
dentro de los ojos
un puñal de plata.
Bajaban al río.
¡Ay, cómo bajaban!
La sangre corría
más fuerte que el agua. |
|---|---|
| MUJER: | Duérmete, clavel,
que el caballo no quiere beber. |
| SUEGRA: | Duérmete, rosal,
que el caballo se pone a llorar. |
| MUJER: | No quiso tocar
la orilla mojada
su belfo caliente
con moscas de plata.
A los montes duros
sólo relinchaba
con el río muerto
sobre la garganta. |

MOTHER-IN-LAW: Go to sleep, rose-bush, the horse begins to cry. Wounded legs, frozen manes, and within the eyes a silver dagger. Down the river they went. Ah, how they went downwards! Blood ran faster than water.

WOMAN: Go to sleep, carnation, the horse will not drink.

MOTHER-IN-LAW: Go to sleep, rose-bush, the horse begins to cry.

WOMAN: His hot muzzle, bearing silver flies, would not touch the wet shore. He would only neigh towards the hard mountains,

¡Ay caballo grande
que no quiso el agua!
¡Ay dolor de nieve,
caballo del alba!

SUEGRA: ¡No vengas! Detente,
cierra la ventana
con ramas de sueños
y sueño de ramas.

MUJER: Mi niño se duerme.

SUEGRA: Mi niño se calla.

MUJER: Caballo, mi niño
tiene una almohada.

SUEGRA: Su cuna de acero.

MUJER: Su colcha de holanda.

SUEGRA: Nana, niño, nana.

with the dead river against his throat. Ah, big horse who would not drink water! Ah, pain of snow, horse of daybreak!

MOTHER-IN-LAW: Do not come! Stop, close the window with a branch of dreams and a dream of branches.

WOMAN: My child falls asleep.

MOTHER-IN-LAW: My child is silent.

WOMAN: Horse, my child has a pillow.

MOTHER-IN-LAW: His cradle of steel.

WOMAN: His coverlet of fine linen.

MUJER: ¡Ay caballo grande
              que no quiso el agua!

SUEGRA: ¡No vengas, no entres!
              Véte a la montaña.
              Por los valles grises
              donde está la jaca.

MUJER (*mirando*):
              Mi niño se duerme.

SUEGRA: Mi niño descansa.

MUJER (*bajito*):
              Duérmete, clavel,
              que el caballo no quiere beber.

SUEGRA (*levantándose y muy bajito*):
              Duérmete, rosal,
              que el caballo se pone a llorar.

(*Bodas de Sangre*, Acto 1)

MOTHER-IN-LAW: Lullaby, child, lullaby.

WOMAN: Ah, big horse who would not drink water!

MOTHER-IN-LAW: Do not come, do not come in! Go to the mountains. Through the grey valleys where the mare is.

WOMAN (*looking*): My child falls asleep.

MOTHER-IN-LAW: My child is resting.

WOMAN (*softly*): Go to sleep, carnation, the horse will not drink.

MOTHER-IN-LAW (*getting up, and very softly*): Go to sleep, rose-bush, the horse begins to cry.

(*Blood Wedding*, Act 1)

MONÓLOGO DE LA LUNA

Cisne redondo en el río,
ojo de las catedrales,
alba fingida en las hojas
soy. ¡No podrán escaparse!
¿Quién se oculta? ¿Quién solloza
por la maleza del valle?
La luna deja un cuchillo
abandonado en el aire,
que siendo acecho de plomo
quiere ser dolor de sangre.
¡Dejadme entrar! ¡Vengo helada
por paredes y cristales!
¡Abrid tejados y pechos
donde pueda calentarme!
¡Tengo frío! Mis cenizas
de soñolientos metales,
buscan la cresta del fuego
por los montes y las calles.
Pero me lleva la nieve
sobre su espalda de jaspe,
y me anega, dura y fría,
el agua de los estanques.
Pues esta noche tendrán
mis mejillas roja sangre,

Monologue of the Moon

I AM the round swan of the river, eye of cathedrals, false dawn on the leaves; they shall not escape! Who is hiding? Who sobs in the thicket of the valley? The moon leaves a knife abandoned in the air, which being ambush of lead wants to be pain of blood. Let me in! I come freezing along walls and window-panes! Open roofs and breasts where I may warm myself! I am cold! My ashes of sleeping metals seek the crest of fire on hills and streets. But the snow carries me on its shoulders of jasper, and the water of the ponds, cold and hard, drowns me. For tonight there will be red blood on my cheeks,

y los juncos agrupados
en los anchos pies del aire.
¡No haya sombra ni emboscada,
que no puedan escaparse!
¡Que quiero entrar en un pecho
para poder calentarme!
¡Un corazón para mí!
¡Caliente!, que se derrame
por los montes de mi pecho;
dejadme entrar, ¡ay, dejadme!
 (*A las ramas.*)
No quiero sombras. Mis rayos
han de entrar en todas partes,
y haya en los troncos oscuros
un rumor de claridades,
para que esta noche tengan
mis mejillas dulce sangre,
y los juncos agrupados
en los anchos pies del aire.
¿Quién se oculta? ¡Afuera digo!
¡No! ¡No podrán escaparse!
Yo haré lucir al caballo
una fiebre de diamante.

(*Bodas de Sangre*, Acto III)

and on the reeds clustered under the wind's broad feet. Let there be
no shadow or cover, for they must not escape! I want to enter a
breast and warm myself! A heart for me! Warm!, that will spread over
the mountains of my breast; let me in, oh, let me! (*To the branches*) I
want no shadow. My rays must penetrate everywhere, and let there
be a murmur of splendours on the dark stems, so that tonight there
may be sweet blood on my cheeks, and on the reeds clustered under
the wind's broad feet. Who is hiding? Out, I say! No! They shall not
escape! I will make the horse gleam with the fever of a diamond.

(*Blood Wedding*, Act III)

MUJER: ERA hermoso jinete,
              y ahora montón de nieve.
              Corrió ferias y montes
              y brazos de mujeres.
              Ahora, musgo de noche
              le corona la frente.

MADRE: Girasol de tu madre,
              espejo de la tierra.
              Que te pongan al pecho
              cruz de amargas adelfas;
              sábana que te cubra
              de reluciente seda,
              y el agua forme un llanto
              entre tus manos quietas.

MUJER: ¡Ay, qué cuatro muchachos
              llegan con hombros cansados!

NOVIA: ¡Ay, qué cuatro galanes
              traen a la muerte por el aire!

MADRE: Vecinas.

WOMAN: He was a handsome horseman, and now he is a heap of
snow. He followed fairs and hills and women's arms. Now, night
moss crowns his forehead.

MOTHER: Your mother's sunflower, mirror of the earth. Let them
place on your chest a cross of bitter oleanders; and over you a sheet
of shining silk, and let water shape a lament between your still
hands.

WOMAN: Ah, four young men come, their shoulders weary!

BRIDE: Ah, four fine young men carrying death through the air!

MOTHER: Neighbours.

NIÑA (*en la puerta*):
Ya los traen.

MADRE:
Es lo mismo,
La cruz, la cruz.

MUJERES:
Dulces clavos,
dulce cruz,
dulce nombre
de Jesús.

NOVIA:
Que la cruz ampare a muertos y vivos.

MADRE:
Vecinas, con un cuchillo,
con un cuchillito,
en un día señalado, entre las dos y las
tres,
se mataron los dos hombres del amor.
Con un cuchillo,
con un cuchillito
que apenas cabe en la mano,
pero que penetra fino
por las carnes asombradas,
y que se para en el sitio

GIRL (*at the door*): They are bringing them now.
MOTHER: Always the same. The cross, the cross.
WOMEN: Sweet nails, sweet cross, sweet name of Jesus.
BRIDE: May the cross protect the dead and the living.
MOTHER: Neighbours: with a knife, with a little knife, on a fateful day, between the hours of two and three, the two men of love killed themselves. With a knife, with a little knife which scarcely fits into the hand, but which penetrates thinly through the astonished

125

donde tiembla enmarañada
la oscura raíz del grito.

NOVIA: Y esto es un cuchillo,
un cuchillito
que apenas cabe en la mano;
pez sin escamas ni río,
para que un día señalado, entre las dos y
    las tres,
con este cuchillo
se queden dos hombres duros
con los labios amarillos.

MADRE: Y apenas cabe en la mano,
pero que penetra frío
por las carnes asombradas
y allí se para, en el sitio
donde tiembla enmarañada
la oscura raíz del grito.

(*Bodas de Sangre*, Final)

flesh, and stops where entangled trembles the dark root of the shriek.

BRIDE: And this is a knife, a little knife which scarcely fits into the hand; fish without scales or river, so that on a fateful day, between the hours of two and three, with this knife two men are left stiff, with their lips turned yellow.

MOTHER: And it scarcely fits into the hand, but it penetrates coldly through the astonished flesh and stops there, at the place where entangled trembles the dark root of the shriek.

(*Blood Wedding*. The end)

(El marido sale y Yerma se dirige a la costura, se pasa la mano por el vientre, alza los brazos en un hermoso bostezo y se sienta a coser.)

¿DE dónde vienes, amor, mi niño?
De la cresta del duro frío.
¿Qué necesitas, amor, mi niño?
La tibia tela de tu vestido.
    (Enhebra la aguja.)
¡Que se agiten las ramas al sol
y salten las fuentes alrededor!
    (Como si hablara con un niño.)
En el patio ladra el perro,
en los árboles canta el viento.
Los bueyes mugen al boyero
y la luna me riza los cabellos.
¿Qué pides, niño, desde tan lejos?
    (Pausa.)
Los blancos montes que hay en tu pecho.
¡Que se agiten las ramas al sol
y salten las fuentes alrededor!

(As the husband leaves, Yerma goes towards her needle-work, passes her hands across her belly, stretches her arms out to yawn widely, and sits down to sew.)

FROM where do you come, my love, my child? From the ridge of hard frost. What do you need, my love, my child? The warm cloth of your dress. (*Threads the needle.*) Let the branches ruffle in the sun and the fountains leap all around! (*As though speaking to a child.*) In the courtyard a dog barks, in the trees the wind sings. The oxen low to the ox-herd and the moon curls my hair. What do you ask for, my child, from so far away? (*Pause.*) The white mountains of your breast. Let the branches ruffle in the sun and the fountains leap all

(*Cosiendo.*)
Te diré, niño mío, que sí,
tronchada y rota soy para ti.
¡Cómo me duele esta cintura
donde tendrás primera cuna!
¿Cuándo, mi niño, vas a venir?
    (*Pausa.*)
Cuando tu carne huela a jazmín.
¡Que se agiten las ramas al sol
y salten las fuentes alrededor!

(*Yerma*, Acto I)

¿Por qué duermes solo, pastor?
En mi colcha de lana
dormirías mejor.
Tu colcha de oscura piedra,
        pastor,
y tu camisa de escarcha,
        pastor,
juncos grises del invierno
en la noche de tu cama.

around! (*Sewing.*) I'll tell you, my child, yes, I am torn and broken
for you. How painful is this waist where you will have your first cra-
dle! When, my child, will you come? (*Pause.*) When your flesh smells
of jasmine-flowers. Let the branches ruffle in the sun and the foun-
tains leap all around!

(*Yerma*, Act I)

Why do you sleep alone, shepherd? In my wool coverlet you would
sleep better. Your coverlet of dark stone, shepherd, and your shirt of
white frost, shepherd, are grey, wintry rushes in the night of your

Los robles ponen agujas,
                pastor,
debajo de tu almohada,
                pastor,
y si oyes voz de mujer
es la rota voz del agua.
                Pastor, pastor.
¿Qué quiere el monte de ti?,
                pastor.
Monte de hierbas amargas,
¿qué niño te está matando?
¡La espina de la retama!

(*Yerma*, Acto 1)

¡Ay, qué prado de pena!
¡Ay, qué puerta cerrada a la hermosura!,
que pido un hijo que sufrir, y el aire
me ofrece dalias de dormida luna.
Estos dos manantiales que yo tengo
de leche tibia son en la espesura
de mi carne dos pulsos de caballo
que hacen latir la rama de mi angustia.

bed. The oak-trees, shepherd, lay needles under your pillow, shepherd, and if you hear womanly voice, it is the broken voice of the water. Shepherd, shepherd. What does the mountain want of you, shepherd? Mountain of bitter grass, what child is killing you? The thorn of the gorse!

(*Yerma*, Act 1)

AH, what a meadow of sorrow! Ah, what a door closed to beauty! I ask to suffer a child, and the air offers me dahlias of sleeping moon. These two fountains that I have of warm milk are in the closeness of my flesh, pulsation of two horses which make the branch of my

¡Ay, pechos ciegos bajo mi vestido!
¡Ay, palomas sin ojos ni blancura!
¡Ay, qué dolor de sangre prisionera
me está clavando avispas en la nuca!
Pero tú has de venir, amor, mi niño,
porque el agua da sal, la tierra fruta,
y nuestro vientre guarda tiernos hijos,
como la nube lleva dulce lluvia.

(Yerma, Acto II)

LLANTO POR IGNACIO SÁNCHEZ MEJÍAS

I

LA COGIDA Y LA MUERTE

A LAS cinco de la tarde.
Eran las cinco en punto de la tarde.
Un niño trajo la blanca sábana
a las cinco de la tarde.
Una espuerta de cal ya prevenida
a las cinco de la tarde.

anguish throb. Ah, blind breasts beneath my dress! Ah, pigeons without eyes or whiteness! Ah, what pain of imprisoned blood is nailing wasps in my neck! But you must come, my love, my child, because the water bears salt, the earth fruit, and our belly holds tender sons, as the cloud carries sweet rain.

(Yerma, Act II)

Lament for Ignacio Sánchez Mejías

I. THE TOSSING AND THE DEATH

AT five in the afternoon. It was exactly five in the afternoon. A boy brought the white sheet *at five in the afternoon.* A frail of lime made

Lo demás era muerte y sólo muerte
a las cinco de la tarde.

El viento se llevó los algodones
a las cinco de la tarde.
Y el óxido sembró cristal y níquel
a las cinco de la tarde.
Ya luchan la paloma y el leopardo
a las cinco de la tarde.
Y un muslo con un asta desolada
a las cinco de la tarde.
Comenzaron los sones de bordón
a las cinco de la tarde.
Las campanas de arsénico y el humo
a las cinco de la tarde.
En las esquinas grupos de silencio
a las cinco de la tarde.
¡Y el toro solo corazón arriba!
a las cinco de la tarde.
Cuando el sudor de nieve fué llegando
a las cinco de la tarde,
cuando la plaza se cubrió de yodo
a las cinco de la tarde,
la muerte puso huevos en la herida

ready *at five in the afternoon*. The rest was death and death alone *at five in the afternoon.*

The wind blew the cotton-wool away *at five in the afternoon.* And the oxide scattered glass and nickel *at five in the afternoon.* Now the dove and the leopard fight *at five in the afternoon.* And a thigh with a desolate horn *at five in the afternoon.* Bourdon sounds struck up *at five in the afternoon.* Arsenic bells and smoke *at five in the afternoon.* At every corner hushed groups *at five in the afternoon.* And the bull alone exultant! *at five in the afternoon.* When the sweat of snow appeared *at five in the afternoon,* when the bull-ring was covered with iodine *at five in the afternoon,* death laid eggs in the wound *at five in the*

a las cinco de la tarde.
A las cinco de la tarde.
A las cinco en punto de la tarde.

Un ataúd con ruedas es la cama
a las cinco de la tarde.
Huesos y flautas suenan en su oído
a las cinco de la tarde.
El toro ya mugía por su frente
a las cinco de la tarde.
El cuarto se irisaba de agonía
a las cinco de la tarde.
A lo lejos ya viene la gangrena
a las cinco de la tarde.
Trompa de lirio por las verdes ingles
a las cinco de la tarde.
Las heridas quemaban como soles
a las cinco de la tarde,
y el gentío rompía las ventanas
a las cinco de la tarde.
A las cinco de la tarde.
¡Ay, qué terribles cinco de la tarde!
¡Eran las cinco en todos los relojes!
¡Eran las cinco en sombra de la tarde!

afternoon. At five in the afternoon. At exactly five in the afternoon.

A coffin on wheels is his bed *at five in the afternoon.* Bones and flutes rung in his ears *at five in the afternoon.* Now the bull bellows on his forehead *at five in the afternoon.* The room became iridescent with agony *at five in the afternoon.* In the distance the gangrene now is coming *at five in the afternoon.* A lily-trumpet in his green groins *at five in the afternoon.* The wounds burned like suns *at five in the afternoon,* and the crowd was breaking windows *at five in the afternoon.* At five in the afternoon. Ah, that dreadful five in the afternoon! It was five by all the clocks! It was the shadow of five in the afternoon!

LA SANGRE DERRAMADA

¡QUE no quiero verla!

Dile a la luna que venga,
que no quiero ver la sangre
de Ignacio sobre la arena.

¡Que no quiero verla!

La luna de par en par.
Caballo de nubes quietas,
y la plaza gris del sueño
con sauces en las barreras.

¡Que no quiero verla!

Que mi recuerdo se quema.
¡Avisad a los jazmines
con su blancura pequeña!

¡Que no quiero verla!

2. THE SPILLED BLOOD

I DO not want to see it!

Tell the moon to come, for I do not want to see Ignacio's blood on the sand.

I do not want to see it!

The moon wide open. Horse of still clouds, and the dream's grey bull-ring with willows in the barriers.

I do not want to see it! For my remembrance burns. Warn the jasmines with their small whiteness!

I do not want to see it!

La vaca del viejo mundo
pasaba su triste lengua
sobre un hocico de sangres
derramadas en la arena,
y los toros de Guisando,
casi muerte y casi piedra,
mugieron como dos siglos
hartos de pisar la tierra.
No.
¡Que no quiero verla!

Por las gradas sube Ignacio
con toda su muerte a cuestas.
Buscaba el amanecer,
y el amanecer no era.
Busca su perfil seguro,
y el sueño lo desorienta.
Buscaba su hermoso cuerpo
y encontró su sangre abierta.
¡No me digáis que la vea!
No quiero sentir el chorro
cada vez con menos fuerza;
ese chorro que ilumina
los tendidos y se vuelca
sobre la pana y el cuero

The cow of the ancient world passed her sad tongue over a snout
full of the blood spilt on the sand, and the bulls of Guisando, partly
death and partly stone, bellow like two centuries weary with tread-
ing the earth. No. I do not want to see it!

Ignacio climbs up the tiers with all his death on his shoulders.
He was seeking the daybreak, and the daybreak did not exist. He
seeks his confident profile, and the dream dims it. He was seeking
his beautiful body, and he encountered his opened blood. Do not
ask me to see it! I do not want to hear the gush slowly weakening;
a gush illuminating the tiers and spilling over the corduroy and the

de muchedumbre sedienta.
¡Quién me grita que me asome!
¡No me digáis que la vea!

No se cerraron sus ojos
cuando vió los cuernos cerca,
pero las madres terribles
levantaron la cabeza.
Y a través de las ganaderías,
hubo un aire de voces secretas
que gritaban a toros celestes,
mayorales de pálida niebla.
No hubo príncipe en Sevilla
que comparársele pueda,
ni espada como su espada
ni corazón tan de veras.
Como un río de leones
su maravillosa fuerza,
y como un torso de mármol
su dibujada prudencia.
Aire de Roma andaluza
le doraba la cabeza
donde su risa era un nardo
de sal y de inteligencia.
¡Qué gran torero en la plaza!

leather of an eager multitude. Who shouts to me to come forward!
Do not ask me to see it!

His eyes did not shut when he saw the horns near, but the terrible mothers lifted their heads. And through the cattle-ranches rose a breeze of secret voices that ranchers of pale mist shouted at celestial bulls. There never was prince in Seville to compare to him, nor a sword like his sword, nor a heart so true. Like a river of lions was his astonishing strength, and like a marble torso his outstanding discretion. An air of Andalusian Rome gilded his head, on which his smile was a tuberose of wit and intelligence. What a great bull-fighter in

¡Qué buen serrano en la sierra!
¡Qué blando con las espigas!
¡Qué duro con las espuelas!
¡Qué tierno con el rocío!
¡Qué deslumbrante en la feria!
¡Qué tremendo con las últimas
banderillas de tiniebla!

Pero ya duerme sin fin.
Ya los musgos y la hierba
abren con dedos seguros
la flor de su calavera.
Y su sangre ya viene cantando:
cantando por marismas y praderas,
resbalando por cuernos ateridos,
vacilando sin alma por la niebla,
tropezando con miles de pezuñas
como una larga, oscura, triste lengua
para formar un charco de agonía
junto al Guadalquivir de las estrellas.
¡Oh blanco muro de España!
¡Oh negro toro de pena!

the ring! What a good countryman in the sierra! How gentle with
the ears of corn! How hard with the spurs! How tender with the
dew! How dazzling at the fair! How tremendous with the final *ban-
derillas*★ of darkness!

But now he sleeps for ever. Now the moss and the grass with
sure fingers unfold the flower of his skull. And now his blood comes
singing: singing through marshes and meadows, sliding down
numbed horns, faltering soulless in the mist, stumbling over a thou-
sand hooves, like a long, dark, sad tongue to form a pool of agony
close to the starry Guadalquivir. Oh, white wall of Spain! Oh, black

---

★ *Banderillas*, thin stick with harpoon-like steel point, adorned with
coloured paper or flags, and placed in pairs in the withers of the bull to
provoke a charge.

¡Oh sangre dura de Ignacio!
¡Oh ruiseñor de sus venas!
No.
¡Que no quiero verla!

Que no hay cáliz que la contenga,
que no hay golondrinas que se la beban,
no hay escarcha de luz que la enfríe,
no hay canto ni diluvio de azucenas,
no hay cristal que la cubra de plata.
No.
¡¡Yo no quiero verla!!

3

CUERPO PRESENTE

LA piedra es una frente donde los sueños gimen
sin tener agua curva ni cipreses helados.
La piedra es una espalda para llevar al tiempo
con árboles de lágrimas y cintas y planetas.

Yo he visto lluvias grises correr hacia las olas,
levantando sus tiernos brazos acribillados,

bull of sorrow! Oh, hard blood of Ignacio! Oh, nightingale of his
veins! No. I do not want to see it!

There is no chalice to hold it, there are no swallows to drink it,
there is no frost of light to cool it, there is no song nor deluge of
lilies, there is no glass that will silver it. No. I will not see it!

3. THE LAID-OUT BODY

THE slab of stone is a forehead where dreams groan deprived of
winding waters and frozen cypresses. The stone is a shoulder to
carry Time, with trees of tears and ribbons and planets.

I have seen grey showers run towards the waves raising their ten-
der riddled arms in order to avoid being caught by the outstretched

para no ser cazadas por la piedra tendida
que desata sus miembros sin empapar la sangre.

Porque la piedra coge simientes y nublados,
esqueletos de alondras y lobos de penumbra;
pero no da sonidos, ni cristales, ni fuego,
sino plazas y plazas y otras plazas sin muros.

Ya está sobre la piedra Ignacio el bien nacido.
Ya se acabó; ¿qué pasa? Contemplad su figura:
la muerte le ha cubierto de pálidos azufres
y le ha puesto cabeza de oscuro minotauro.

Ya se acabó. La lluvia penetra por su boca.
El aire corno loco deja su pecho hundido,
y el Amor, empapado con lágrimas de nieve,
se calienta en la cumbre de las ganaderías.

¿Qué dicen? Un silencio con hedores reposa.
Estamos con un cuerpo presente que se esfuma,
con una forma clara que tuvo ruiseñores
y la vemos llenarse de agujeros sin fondo.

---

stone which loosens their limbs and does not absorb the blood.

For the stone gathers seeds and clouds, lark's skeletons and
wolves of twilight; but it gives no sound, nor crystals, nor fire, only
bull-rings and bull-rings and more bull-rings without walls.

Now Ignacio the well-born lies on the stone. It is all over; what
is happening? Look at his figure: death has covered it with pale sul-
phurs, and placed on him the head of a dark minotaur.

It is all over. Rain enters through his mouth. Air, in a frenzy,
leaves his sunken chest, and Love, soaked with tears of snow, warms
itself above the herds.

What are they saying? A stenching silence settles down. We are
here with a laid-out body which is fading away, with a noble form
which had nightingales, and we see it being filled with bottomless
holes.

¿Quién arruga el sudario? ¡No es verdad lo que dice!
Aquí no canta nadie, ni llora en el rincón,
ni pica las espuelas, ni espanta la serpiente:
aquí no quiero más que los ojos redondos
para ver ese cuerpo sin posible descanso.

Yo quiero ver aquí los hombres de voz dura.
Los que doman caballos y dominan los ríos:
los hombres que les suena el esqueleto y cantan
con una boca llena de sol y pedernales.

Aquí quiero yo verlos. Delante de la piedra.
Delante de este cuerpo con las riendas quebradas.
Yo quiero que me enseñen dónde está la salida
para este capitán atado por la muerte.

Yo quiero que me enseñen un llanto como un río
que tenga dulces nieblas y profundas orillas,
para llevar el cuerpo de Ignacio y que se pierda
sin escuchar el doble resuello de los toros.

Who is ruffling the shroud? It is not true what he says! Nobody
is to sing here, or weep in the corner, or prick his spurs, or frighten
the snake: Here I want only my round eyes to see this body without
a possibility of rest.

Here I want to see those men of strong voice. Those who break
in horses and master rivers: those men whose skeletons rattle and
who sing with mouths full of sun and flints.

Here I want to see them. Before this stone. Before this body with
broken reins. I want them to show me where there is a way out for
this captain bound by death.

I want them to show me a lament like a river with sweet mists
and steep banks to bear the body of Ignacio, and let him disappear
without hearing the double snorting of the bulls.

Que se pierda en la plaza redonda de la luna
que finge cuando niña doliente res inmóvil;
que se pierda en la noche sin canto de los peces
y en la maleza blanca del humo congelado.

No quiero que le tapen la cara con pañuelos
para que se acostumbre con la muerte que lleva.
Vete, Ignacio. No sientas el caliente bramido.
Duerme, vuela, reposa: ¡También se muere el mar!

4

ALMA AUSENTE

No te conoce el toro ni la higuera,
ni caballos ni hormigas de tu casa.
No te conoce el niño ni la tarde
porque te has muerto para siempre.

No te conoce el lomo de la piedra,
ni el raso negro donde te destrozas.
No te conoce tu recuerdo mudo
porque te has muerto para siempre.

Let him disappear in the round bull-ring of the moon, which
feigns when young a mournful, quiet bull; let him disappear in the
night without fishes' songs and in the white thicket of frozen smoke.

I do not want his face to be covered with handkerchiefs, I want
him to get used to the death he carries. Go, Ignacio: Forget the hot
bellowing. Sleep, soar, rest: Even the sea dies!

4. ABSENT SOUL

THE bull does not know you nor the fig-tree, nor horses nor ants of
your house. The child does not know you nor the afternoon,
because you have died for ever.

The back of the stone slab does not know you nor the black satin
in which you crumble. Your silent remembrance does not know you
because you have died for ever.

El otoño vendrá con caracolas,
uva de niebla y montes agrupados,
pero nadie querrá mirar tus ojos
porque te has muerto para siempre.

Porque te has muerto para siempre,
como todos los muertos de la Tierra,
como todos los muertos que se olvidan
en un montón de perros apagados.

No te conoce nadie. No. Pero yo te canto.
Yo canto para luego tu perfil y tu gracia.
La madurez insigne de tu conocimiento.
Tu apetencia de muerte y el gusto de su boca.
La tristeza que tuvo tu valiente alegría.

Tardará mucho tiempo en nacer, si es que nace,
un andaluz tan claro, tan rico de aventura.
Yo canto su elegancia con palabras que gimen
y recuerdo una brisa triste por los olivos.

The autumn will come with trumpet-shells,* grapes of mist, and clustered hills, but no one will want to look into your eyes because you have died for ever.

Because you have died for ever, like all the dead of the Earth, like all the dead who are forgotten in a heap of obscure dogs.

Nobody knows you. No. But I sing of you. I sing for posterity of your profile and your grace. The noble maturity of your understanding. Your appetite for death and the taste of its mouth. The sadness inherent in your valiant gaiety.

Not for a long time will be born, if ever, an Andalusian so noble, so rich in adventure. I sing of his elegance in words that moan, and I remember a sad breeze among the olive-trees.

---

* *Caracola*, conch-shell. The shepherds on the hills overlooking Granada use a conch-shell horn to communicate with each other, and in the autumn, with the movement of flocks from hill to plain, the sound of the *caracolas* is heard more insistently.

GACELA DE LA TERRIBLE PRESENCIA

Yo quiero que el agua se quede sin cauce.
Yo quiero que el viento se quede sin valles.

Quiero que la noche se quede sin ojos
y mi corazón sin la flor del oro;

que los bueyes hablen con las grandes hojas
y que la lombriz se muera de sombra;

que brillen los dientes de la calavera
y los amarillos inunden la seda.

Puedo ver el duelo de la noche herida
luchando enroscada con el mediodía.

Resisto un ocaso de verde veneno
y los arcos rotos donde sufre el tiempo.

Gacela * *of the Terrible Presence*

I WANT the water to lose its course. I want the wind to lose its valleys.

I want the night to lose its eyes, and my heart its gold-flower; I want the oxen to speak with the great leaves, and the earthworm to die of gloom;

I want the skull's teeth to shine, and yellows to flood the silk. I can see the duel of the wounded night wrestling entwined with midday.

I resist a sunset of green poison, and the broken arches where Time suffers.

---

* An Arabic poetical form, usually of an erotic character.

Pero no ilumines tu limpio desnudo
como un negro cactus abierto en los juncos.

Déjame en un ansia de oscuros planetas,
pero no me enseñes tu cintura fresca.

GACELA DE LA MUERTE OSCURA

Quiero dormir el sueño de las manzanas,
alejarme del tumulto de los cementerios.
Quiero dormir el sueño de aquel niño
que quería cortarse el corazón en alta mar.

No quiero que me repitan que los muertos no pierden
    la sangre;
que la boca podrida sigue pidiendo agua.
No quiero enterarme de los martirios que da la hierba,
ni de la luna con boca de serpiente
que trabaja antes del amanecer.

But do not make your pure nakedness resplendent like a black
cactus unfolded among the reeds.

Leave me in a dread of obscure planets, but do not show me your
serene waist.

Gacela *of the Dark Death*

I WANT to sleep the sleep of apples, I want to leave the tumult of
cemeteries. I want to sleep the sleep of that child who wanted to cut
his heart on the high seas.

I do not want to hear again that corpses do not lose their blood;
that the rotting mouth keeps asking for water. I do not want to
know what torments grass bestows, nor do I want to know of the
moon with a serpent's mouth which works before daybreak.

Quiero dormir un rato,
un rato, un minuto, un siglo;
pero que todos sepan que no he muerto;
que hay un establo de oro en mis labios;
que soy el pequeño amigo del viento Oeste;
que soy la sombra inmensa de mis lágrimas.

Cúbreme por la aurora con un velo,
porque me arrojará puñados de hormigas,
y moja con agua dura mis zapatos
para que resbale la pinza de su alacrán.

Porque quiero dormir el sueño de las manzanas
para aprender un llanto que me limpie de tierra;
porque quiero vivir con aquel niño oscuro
que quería cortarse el corazón en alta mar.

I want to sleep for a while, a while, a minute, a century, but all must know that I have not died, that there is a stable of gold in my lips, that I am the little friend of the West wind, that I am the immense shadow of my tears.

Cover me with a veil at dawn, because it will throw fistfuls of ants at me, and steep my shoes in hard water so that its scorpion's pincers may slide.

Because I want to sleep the sleep of apples, to learn a lament that will cleanse me of earth; because I want to live with that sad child who wanted to cut his heart on the high seas.

GACELA DE LA HUIDA

Me he perdido muchas veces por el mar
con el oído lleno de flores recién cortadas,
con la lengua llena de amor y de agonía.
Muchas veces me he perdido por el mar,
como me pierdo en el corazón de algunos niños.

No hay nadie que al dar un beso
no sienta la sonrisa de la gente sin rostro,
ni nadie que al tocar un recién nacido
olvide las inmóviles calaveras de caballo.

Porque las rosas buscan en la frente
un duro paisaje de hueso
y las manos del hombre no tienen más sentido
que imitar a las raíces bajo la tierra.

Como me pierdo en el corazón de algunos niños,
me he perdido muchas veces por el mar.
Ignorante del agua voy buscando
una muerte de luz que me consuma.

Gacela of the Flight

Many times I have lost myself in the sea with my ears full of freshly cut flowers, with my tongue full of love and agony. Many times I have lost myself in the sea as I lose myself in the heart of some children.

There is no one who, in giving a kiss, does not feel the smile of faceless people; and no one who, in touching a newborn child, forgets the motionless skull of horses.

Because roses search in the forehead for a hard landscape of bone, and the hands of man have no other object than to imitate the roots under the earth.

As I lose myself in the heart of some children, many times I have lost myself in the sea. Unaware of the water, I go searching a death in which light consumes me.

CASIDA DEL HERIDO POR EL AGUA

QUIERO bajar al pozo,
quiero subir los muros de Granada,
para mirar el corazón pasado
por el punzón oscuro de las aguas.

El niño herido gemía
con una corona de escarcha.
Estanques, aljibes y fuentes
levantaban al aire sus espadas.
¡Ay, qué furia de amor, qué hiriente filo,
qué nocturno rumor, qué muerte blanca!
¡Qué desiertos de luz iban hundiendo
los arenales de la madrugada!
El niño estaba solo
con la ciudad dormida en la garganta.
Un surtidor que viene de los sueños
lo defiende del hambre de las algas.
El niño y su agonía, frente a frente,
eran dos verdes lluvias enlazadas.

Casida ★ *of the One Wounded by the Water*

I WANT to go down the well, I want to go up the walls of Granada,
to look at the heart pierced by the dark bodkin of the water.

The wounded child groaned with a crown of white frost; ponds,
cisterns, and fountains raised their swords to the air. Ah, what fury of
love! What stabbing edge, what nocturnal murmur, what white
death! What deserts of light sunk in the sands of daybreak! The child
was alone with the sleeping city in his throat. A fountain arising
from dreams protects him from the hunger of sea-weeds. The child
and his agony, face to face, were two interlaced green showers. The

---

★ An Arabic poetical form, usually on an amorous theme.

El niño se tendía por la tierra
y su agonía se curvaba.

Quiero bajar al pozo,
quiero morir mi muerte a bocanadas,
quiero llenar mi corazón de musgo,
para ver al herido por el agua.

CASIDA DEL LLANTO

HE cerrado mi balcón
porque no quiero oír el llanto,
pero por detrás de los grises muros
no se oye otra cosa que el llanto.

Hay muy pocos ángeles que canten,
hay muy pocos perros que ladren,
mil violines caben en la palma de mi mano.

Pero el llanto es un perro inmenso,
el llanto es un ángel inmenso,
el llanto es un violín inmenso,

child was stretching himself on the earth and his agony curved itself round.

I want to go down the well, I want to die my death in gulps, I want to fill my heart with moss, to see the one wounded by the water.

Casida *of the Weeping*

I HAVE shut my balcony window because I do not want to hear the weeping, yet from behind the grey walls nothing else is heard but the weeping.

There are very few angels that sing, there are very few dogs that bark, a thousand violins fit into the palm of my hand.

But the weeping is an immense dog, the weeping is an immense

las lágrimas amordazan al viento,
y no se oye otra cosa que el llanto.

CASIDA DE LOS RAMOS

Por las arboledas del Tamarit
han venido los perros de plomo
a esperar que se caigan los ramos,
a esperar que se quiebren ellos solos.

El Tamarit tiene un manzano
con una manzana de sollozos.
Un ruiseñor apaga los suspiros
y un faisán los ahuyenta por el polvo.

Pero los ramos son alegres,
los ramos son como nosotros.
No piensan en la lluvia y se han dormido,
como si fueran árboles, de pronto.

angel, the weeping is an immense violin, tears muffle the wind, and nothing else is heard but the weeping.

Casida *of the Branches*

Along the groves of the Tamarit leaden dogs have come to wait for the branches to fall, to wait for them to break by themselves.

The Tamarit has an apple-tree with an apple of sobs. A nightingale hushes the sighs, and a pheasant drives them away through the dust.

But the branches are happy, the branches are like ourselves. They have no thought for the rain, and they have fallen asleep as if they were trees, suddenly.

Sentados con el agua en las rodillas
dos valles esperaban al otoño.
La penumbra con paso de elefante
empujaba las ramas y los troncos.

Por las arboledas del Tamarit
hay muchos niños de velado rostro
a esperar que se caigan mis ramos,
a esperar que se quiebren ellos solos.

CASIDA DE LA MUJER TENDIDA

Verte desnuda es recordar la Tierra.
La Tierra lisa, limpia de caballos.
La Tierra sin un junco, forma pura,
cerrada al porvenir: confín de plata.

Verte desnuda es comprender el ansia
de la lluvia que busca débil talle,
o la fiebre del mar de inmenso rostro
sin encontrar la luz de su mejilla.

Seated, with water to the knees, two valleys await the autumn. Dusk, with the step of an elephant, was pushing branches and tree-trunks.

Along the groves of the Tamarit there are many children with veiled face to wait for my branches to fall, to wait for them to break by themselves.

Casida *of the Reclining Woman*

To see you naked is to remember the earth. The smooth earth, empty of horses. The earth without reeds, pure shape closed to the future: horizon of silver.

To see you naked is to understand the anxiety of rain seeking a frail waist, or the feverishness of a sea of immense countenance unable to find the light of its own cheek.

La sangre sonará por las alcobas
y vendrá con espadas fulgurantes,
pero tú no sabrás dónde se ocultan
el corazón de sapo o la violeta.

Tu vientre es una lucha de raíces
y tus labios un alba sin contorno.
Bajo las rosas tibias de la cama
los muertos gimen esperando turno.

CASIDA DE LA ROSA

LA rosa
no buscaba la aurora:
casi eterna en su ramo,
buscaba otra cosa.

La rosa,
no buscaba ni ciencia ni sombra:
confín de carne y sueño,
buscaba otra cosa.

Blood will ring through alcoves and will come with flaming swords, but you will not know where the toad's heart or the violet is hidden.

Your belly is a wrestling of roots, your lips are a daybreak without contour. Under the cool roses of the bed moan the dead, waiting their turn.

Casida *of the Rose*

THE rose did not seek the daybreak: almost eternal on its bough, it sought another thing.

The rose did not seek knowledge or shade: boundary of flesh and dream, it sought another thing.

La rosa,
no buscaba la rosa.
Inmóvil por el cielo
buscaba otra cosa.

CASIDA DE LAS PALOMAS OSCURAS

Por las ramas del laurel
vi dos palomas oscuras.
La una era el sol,
la otra la luna.
«Vecinitas,» les dije:
«¿Dónde está mi sepultura?»
«En mi cola,» dijo el sol.
«En mi garganta,» dijo la luna.
Y yo que estaba caminando
con la tierra por la cintura
vi dos águilas de nieve
y una muchacha desnuda.
La una era la otra
y la muchacha era ninguna.
«Aguilitas,» les dije:

The rose did not seek the rose. Motionless in the sky it sought another thing.

Casida *of the Dark Pigeons*

In the branches of the bay-tree I saw two dark pigeons. One was the sun, the other the moon. 'Little neighbours,' I said to them, 'where is my grave?' 'In my tail,' said the sun. 'In my throat,' said the moon. And I who was walking with the earth round my waist, saw two eagles of snow and a naked girl. One was the other and the girl was neither. 'Little eagles,' I said to them, 'where is my

«¿Dónde está mi sepultura?»
«En mi cola,» dijo el sol.
«En mi garganta,» dijo la luna.
Por las ramas del laurel
vi dos palomas desnudas.
La una era la otra
y las dos eran ninguna.

CADA CANCIÓN

CADA canción
es un remanso
del amor.

Cada lucero,
un remanso
del tiempo.
Un nudo
del tiempo.

Y cada suspiro
un remanso
del grito.

tail,' said the sun. 'In my throat,' said the moon. In the branches of the bay-tree I saw two naked pigeons. One was the other and both were neither.

Each Song . . .

EACH song is love's stillness.
  Each star is time's stillness. A knot of time.
  Each sigh is the stillness of the shriek.

CANTO NOCTURNO DE LOS
MARINEROS ANDALUCES

De Cádiz a Gibraltar
¡qué buen caminito!
El mar conoce mi paso
por los suspiros.

¡Ay, muchacha, muchacha,
cuánto barco en el puerto de Málaga!

De Cádiz a Sevilla
¡cuántos limoncitos!
El limonar me conoce
por los suspiros.

¡Ay, muchacha, muchacha,
cuánto barco en el puerto de Málaga!

De Sevilla a Carmona
no hay un solo cuchillo.
La media luna, corta,
y el aire pasa, herido.

Nocturnal Song of the Andalusian Sailors

From Cádiz to Gibraltar, how good the path! The sea knows my passing by the sighs.

Ah, lass, lass, how full of boats is the port of Málaga!

From Cádiz to Seville, how full of little lemons! The lemon grove knows me by the sighs.

Ah, lass, lass, how full of boats is the port of Málaga!

From Seville to Carmona there is not one knife, the half moon cuts, and the air passes, wounded.

¡Ay, muchacho, muchacho,
que las olas me llevan mi caballo!

Por las salinas muertas
yo te olvidé, amor mío.
El que quiera un corazón
que pregunte por mi olvido.

¡Ay, muchacho, muchacho,
que las olas se llevan mi caballo!

Cádiz, que te cubre el mar,
no avances por ese sitio.
Sevilla, ponte de pie
para no ahogarte en el río.

¡Ay, muchacha!
¡Ay, muchacho!
¡Qué buen caminito!
Cuánto barco en el puerto
y en la plaza ¡qué frío!

Ah, lad, lad, the waves bear away my horse!

Along the deserted salt-mines I forgot you, my love. Whoever
wants a heart, let him ask for my forgetfulness.

Ah, lad, lad, the waves carry away my horse!

Cádiz, the sea drowns you, do not proceed this way. Seville, stand
up, or you will drown in the river.

Ah, lass! Ah, lad! How good the path! How full of boats is the
harbour, and in the square, how cold!

NORMA

NORMA de seno y cadera
bajo la rama tendida;
antigua y recién nacida
virtud de la primavera.
Ya mi desnudo quisiera
ser dalia de tu destino,
abeja, rumor o vino
de tu número y locura;
pero mi amor busca pura
locura de brisa y trino.

Norm

NORM of breast and hip under the bough outstretched; ancient and
new-born virtue of spring. My nakedness would now be dahlia of
your destiny, bee, murmur or wine of your number and folly; but
my love seeks pure folly of breeze and trill.

ADÁN

ARBOL de sangre moja la mañana
por donde gime la recién parida.
Su voz deja cristales en la herida
y un gráfico de hueso en la ventana.

Mientras la luz que viene fija y gana
blancas metas de fábula que olvida
el tumulto de venas en la huida
hacia el turbio frescor de la manzana.

Adán sueña en la fiebre de la arcilla
un niño que se acerca galopando
por el doble latir de su mejilla.

Pero otro Adán oscuro está soñando
neutra luna de piedra sin semilla
donde el niño de luz se irá quemando.

Adam

MORNING by tree of blood is moistened
where the newly-delivered woman groans.
Her voice leaves crystals in the wound
and in the windows a print of bones.

While the light comes in secure and gains
white boundaries of oblivious fable
in the rush from the turmoil of the veins
towards the clouded coolness of the apple.

Adam dreams in the fever of clay
of a child which draws nearer galloping,
with the double throb of his cheek its way.

But another obscure Adam sleeping
dreams neuter seedless stone moon far away
where the child of light will be kindling.

Juego y teoría del duende

✎

Theory and Function
of the *Duende*

Juego y teoría del duende

EL QUE está en la piel de toro extendida entre los Júcar, Guadalfeo, Sil o Pisuerga (no quiero citar a los caudales junto a las ondas color melena de león que agita el Plata), oye decir con medida frecuencia: «Esto tiene mucho duende.» Manuel Torre, gran artista del pueblo andaluz, decía a uno que cantaba: «Tú tienes voz, tú sabes los estilos, pero no triunfarás nunca, porque tú no tienes duende.»

En toda Andalucía, roca de Jaén o caracola de Cádiz, la gente habla constantemente del duende y lo descubre en cuanto sale con instinto eficaz. El maravilloso cantaor *El Lebrijano*. creador de la Debla, decía: «Los días que yo canto con duende no hay quien pueda conmigo»; la vieja bailarina gitana *La Malena* exclamó un día oyendo tocar a Brailowsky un fragmento de Bach: «¡Olé! ¡Eso tiene duende!», y estuvo aburrida con Gluck y con Brahms y con Darius Milhaud. Y Manuel Torre, el hombre de mayor cultura en la sangre que he conocido, dijo, escuchando al propio Falla su *Nocturno del Generalife*, esta espléndida frase: «Todo lo que tiene sonidos negros tiene duende.» Y no hay verdad más grande.

Estos sonidos negros son el misterio, las raíces que se clavan en el limo que todos conocemos, que todos ignoramos, pero de donde nos llega lo que es sustancial en el arte. Sonidos negros dijo el hombre popular de España y coincidió con Goethe, que hace la definición del duende al hablar de Paganini, diciendo: «Poder misterioso que todos sienten y que ningún filósofo explica.»

Así, pues, el duende es un poder y no un obrar, es un luchar y no un pensar. Yo he oído decir a un viejo maestro guitarrista: «El duende no está en la garganta; el duende sube por dentro desde la planta de los pies.» Es decir, no es

Theory and Function of the *Duende* ★

ANYONE travelling in that stretched bull-hide between the Júcar, the Guadalete, the Sil, or the Pisuerga rivers [...], would sooner or later hear the expression: 'This has much *duende*.' Manuel Torre, a great Andalusian artist, on one occasion said to a singer: 'You have voice, you have style, but you will never be a success because you have no *duende*.'

All though Andalusia, from the rock of Jaén to the shell of Cádiz, people constantly speak of the *duende*, and recognize it with unfailing instinct when it appears. The wonderful flamenco singer *El Lebrijano*, creator of the *Debla*,† said: 'When I sing with *duende* nobody can equal me.' The old gipsy dancer *La Malena* exclaimed once on hearing Brailowsky play Bach: 'Olé! This has *duende*!', yet she was bored by Gluck, Brahms, and Darius Milhaud. And Manuel Torre, a man with more culture in his veins than anybody I have known, when listening to Falla playing his own 'Nocturno del Generalife', made this splendid pronouncement: 'All that has dark sounds has *duende*.' And there is no greater truth.

These 'dark sounds' are the mystery, the roots thrusting into the fertile loam known to all of us, ignored by all of us, but from which we get what is real in art. Torre here agrees with Goethe who defined the *duende* when he attributed to Paganini 'a mysterious power that everyone feels but that no philosopher has explained'.

Thus the *duende* is a power and not a behaviour, it is a struggle and not a concept. I have heard an old guitarist master say: 'The *duende* is not in the throat; the *duende* surges up from the soles of the feet.' Which means that it is not a

---

★ A lecture delivered by Lorca in Buenos Aires and Montevideo in 1933.
† *Debla*, a variant of the Andalusian *cante jondo* (deep-song).

cuestión de facultad, sino de verdadero estilo vivo; es decir, de sangre; es decir, de viejísima cultura, de creación en acto.

Este «poder misterioso que todos sienten y que ningún filósofo explica» es, en suma, el espíritu de la tierra, el mismo duende que abrasó el corazón de Nietzsche, que lo buscaba en sus formas exteriores sobre el puente Rialto o en la música de Bizet, sin encontrarlo y sin saber que el duende que él perseguía había saltado de los misterios griegos a las bailarinas de Cádiz o al dionisíaco grito degollado de la siguiriya de Silverio.

Así, pues, no quiero que nadie confunda el duende con el demonio teológico de la duda, al que Lutero, con un sentimiento báquico, le arrojó un frasco de tinta en Nuremberg, ni con el diablo católico, destructor y poco inteligente, que se disfraza de perra para entrar en los conventos, ni con el mono parlante que lleva el Malgesí de Cervantes, en la comedia *[La casa] de los celos y selvas de Ardenia*.

No. El duende de que hablo, oscuro y estremecido, es descendiente de aquel alegrísimo demonio de Sócrates, mármol y sal que lo arañó indignado el día en que tomó la cicuta, y del otro melancólico demonillo de Descartes, pequeño como almendra verde, que, harto de círculos y líneas, salió por los canales para oír cantar a los marineros borrachos.

Todo hombre, todo artista llámese Nietzsche o Cézanne, cada escala★ que sube en la torre de su perfección es a costa de la lucha que sostiene con su duende, no con un ángel, como se ha dicho, ni con su musa. Es preciso hacer esa distinción, fundamental para la raíz de la obra.

★ Older texts began this sentence 'Todo hombre, todo artista llamará Nietzsche, cada escala . . .'. Gili's rendering, which we have updated, was 'Every step that a man, or as Nietzsche would say an artist, takes . . .' [Ed.]

matter of ability, but of real live form; of blood; of ancient culture; of creative action.

This 'mysterious power that everyone feels but that no philosopher has explained' is in fact the spirit of the earth. It is the same *duende* that gripped* the heart of Nietzsche, who had been seeking its external forms on the Rialto Bridge or in the music of Bizet without ever finding it or being aware that the *duende* he pursued had jumped from the Greek mysteries to the dancers of Cádiz or the broken Dionysiac cry of Silverio's *seguiriya*.†

I do not want anybody to confuse the *duende* with Luther's theological daemon of doubt, at whom with a Bacchic touch he flung an inkpot in Nuremberg; nor with the Catholic daemon, destructive and not very intelligent, who disguises himself as a bitch in order to enter convents, nor with the talking monkey carried by Malgesí in Cervantes's comedy *[The House] of the Forests and Jealousies of Ardennes*.

No. The dark and quivering *duende* that I am talking about is a descendant of the merry daemon of Socrates, all marble and salt, who angrily scratched his master on the day he drank hemlock; a descendant also of Descartes' melancholy daemon, small as a green almond, who, tired of lines and circles, went out along the canals to hear the drunken sailors sing.

Every man, every artist, whether his name is Nietzsche or Cézanne, takes a step towards the tower of his perfection at the cost of the struggle he maintains with a *duende*, not with an angel, as has been said, and not with a muse. It is necessary to draw this fundamental distinction in order to arrive at the root of any work.

---

* Translating *abrazó*. Modern texts read *abrasó*, 'scorched'. [Ed.]

† Refers to Silverio Franconetti, an Italian singer who in Andalusia cultivated the *cante jondo*. The *seguiriya* is a development of this.

El ángel guía y regala como San Rafael, defiende y evita como San Miguel, y previene como San Gabriel.

El ángel deslumbra, pero vuela sobre la cabeza del hombre, está por encima, derrama su gracia, y el hombre, sin ningún esfuerzo, realiza su obra o su simpatía o su danza. El ángel del camino de Damasco y el que entra por las rendijas del balconcillo de Asís, o el que sigue los pasos de Enrique Susón, *ordenan* y no hay modo de oponerse a sus luces, porque agitan sus alas de acero en el ambiente del predestinado.

La musa dicta, y, en algunas ocasiones, sopla. Puede relativamente poco, porque ya está lejana y tan cansada (yo la he visto dos veces), que tuvieron que ponerle medio corazón de mármol. Los poetas de musa oyen voces y no saben dónde, pero son de la musa que los alienta y a veces se los merienda. Como en el caso de Apollinaire, gran poeta destruido por la horrible musa con que lo pintó el divino angélico Rousseau. La musa despierta la inteligencia, trae paisajes de columnas y falso sabor de laureles, y la inteligencia es muchas veces la enemiga de la poesía, porque limita demasiado, porque eleva al poeta en un trono de agudas aristas y le hace olvidar que de pronto se lo pueden comer las hormigas o le puede caer en la cabeza una gran langosta de arsénico, contra la cual no pueden las musas que viven en los monóculos o en la rosa de tibia laca del pequeño salón.

Angel y musa vienen de fuera; el ángel da luces y la musa da formas (Hesíodo aprendió de ella). Pan de oro o pliegue de túnica, el poeta recibe normas en su bosquecillo de laureles. En cambio, al duende hay que despertarlo en las últimas habitaciones de la sangre. Y rechazar al ángel, y dar un

The angel guides and endows with gifts like St Raphael, or defends and wards off like St Michael, or warns like St Gabriel.

The angel may dazzle, but he merely hovers over the head of man; he bestows his graces, and man quite effortlessly achieves his work, his sympathy, or his dance. The angel on the road to Damascus and the one who entered through the lattice of the little window at Assisi, or the one who followed the steps of Heinrich Suso, is an angel that *commands*, and no one can resist his radiance because he moves his steel wings in the ambit of the elect.

The muse dictates and, occasionally, inspires. There is relatively little she can do, for she is by now distant and so weary – I have seen her twice – that I had to strengthen her with half a heart of marble. The muse-inspired poets hear voices without knowing where they come from; they come from the muse, who encourages them and sometimes swallows them up. Such was the case of Apollinaire, a great poet destroyed by the horrible muse with whom the magnificent and angelic Rousseau painted him. The muse arouses the intellect, and brings colonnaded landscapes and a false taste of laurel. Very often intellect is poetry's enemy because it is too much given to imitation,* because it lifts the poet to a throne of sharp edges and makes him oblivious of the fact that he may suddenly be devoured by ants, or a great arsenic lobster may fall on his head. Against all this the muses who appear in monocles or among the faintly warm lacquer-roses of a little salon are powerless.

Angel and muse come from without; the angel gives radiance, the muse gives precepts (Hesiod learned from her). Gold leaf or fold of tunics, the poet receives his norms in his coppice of laurels. On the other hand, the *duende* has to be

---

* Translating the old text, *porque imita demasiado*. The modern reading *limita* means 'because it is too limiting'. [Ed.]

puntapié a la musa, y perder el miedo a la fragancia de violetas que exhala la poesía del siglo XVIII, y al gran telescopio en cuyos cristales se duerme la musa enferma de límites.

La verdadera lucha es con el duende.

Se saben los caminos para buscar a Dios, desde el modo bárbaro del eremita al modo sutil del místico. Con una torre como Santa Teresa, o con tres caminos como San Juan de la Cruz. Y aunque tengamos que clamar con voz de Isaías: «Verdaderamente tú eres Dios escondido», al fin y al cabo Dios manda al que lo busca sus primeras espinas de fuego.

Para buscar al duende no hay mapa ni ejercicio. Solo se sabe que quema la sangre como un trópico de vidrios, que agota, que rechaza toda la dulce geometría aprendida, que rompe los estilos, que se apoya en el dolor humano que no tiene consuelo, que hace que Goya, maestro en los grises, en los platas y en los rosas de la mejor pintura inglesa, pinte con las rodillas y los puños con horribles negros de betún; o que desnuda a Mosén Cinto Verdaguer en el frío de los Pirineos, o lleva a Jorge Manrique a esperar a la muerte en el páramo de Ocaña, o viste con un traje verde de saltimbanqui el cuerpo delicado de Rimbaud, o pone ojos de pez muerto al conde Lautréamont en la madrugada del *boulevard*.

Los grandes artistas del sur de España, gitanos o flamencos, ya canten, ya bailen, ya toquen, saben que no es posible ninguna emoción sin la llegada del duende. Ellos engañan a la gente y pueden dar sensación de duende sin haberlo, como os engañan todos los días autores o pintores o modistas literarios sin duende; pero basta fijarse un poco, y no dejarse llevar por la indiferencia, para descubrir la trampa y hacerles huir con su burdo artificio.

---

* Jacint Verdaguer, Catalan poet, a leading figure of the Catalan Renaixença, or literary renaissance of the nineteenth century. Wrote lyric poetry and two great epic poems, *L'Atlàntida* and *Canigó*, hence the Pyrenean reference in the present context.

roused in the very cells of the blood. We must repel the angel, and kick out the muse, and lose our fear of the violet fragrance irradiating from eighteenth-century poetry, and of the great telescope in whose lenses sleeps the confining, ailing muse.

The real struggle is with the *duende*.

One knows how to seek God, whether it be by the rough ways of the hermit or by the subtlety of the mystic; with a tower like St Theresa's, or with the three pathways of St John of the Cross. And even if we have to exclaim with Isaiah's voice: 'Truly thou art the hidden God,' ultimately God sends his first thorns of fire to whoever seeks him.

To help us seek the *duende* there is neither map nor discipline. All one knows is that it burns the blood like powdered glass, that it exhausts, that it rejects all the sweet geometry one has learned, that it breaks with all styles, that it compels Goya, master of greys, silvers, and of those pinks in the best English paintings, to paint with his knees and with his fists horrible bitumen blacks; or that it leaves Mossen Cinto Verdaguer* naked in the cold air of the Pyrenees; or that it takes Jorge Manrique† to wait for death in the wilderness of Ocaña; or that it dresses the delicate body of Rimbaud in an acrobat's green suit; or that it puts the eyes of a dead fish on Count Lautréamont in the early morning Boulevard.

The great artists of Southern Spain, gipsy or flamenco, whether they sing or dance or play, know that no real emotion is possible unless there is *duende*. They may even deceive an audience by giving the impression of possessing *duende*, in the same manner as one is deceived every day by writers, painters, or literary fashions without *duende*; but if one looks closely and is not misled by being inattentive, the fraud will soon be discovered and the *duende*-artifice put to flight.

† Fifteenth-century Spanish poet, famous for his *Coplas* on the death of his father.

Una vez, la «cantaora» andaluza Pastora Pavón, *La Niña de los Peines*, sombrío genio hispánico, equivalente en capacidad de fantasía a Goya o a Rafael el *Gallo*, cantaba en una tabernilla de Cádiz. Jugaba con su voz de sombra, con su voz de estaño fundido, con su voz cubierta de musgo, y se la enredaba en la cabellera o la mojaba en manzanilla o la perdía por unos jarales oscuros y lejanísimos. Pero nada; era inútil. Los oyentes permanecían callados.

Allí estaba Ignacio Espeleta, hermoso como una tortuga romana, a quien preguntaron una vez: «¿Cómo no trabajas?»; y él, con una sonrisa digna de Argantonio, respondió: «¿Cómo voy a trabajar, si soy de Cádiz?»

Allí estaba Eloísa, la caliente aristócrata, ramera de Sevilla, descendiente directa de Soledad Vargas, que en el treinta no se quiso casar con un Rothschild porque no la igualaba en sangre. Allí estaban los Floridas, que la gente cree carniceros, pero que en realidad son sacerdotes milenarios que siguen sacrificando toros a Gerión, y en un ángulo, el imponente ganadero don Pablo Murube, con aire de máscara cretense. Pastora Pavón terminó de cantar en medio del silencio. Solo, y con sarcasmo, un hombre pequeñito, de esos hombrines bailarines que salen, de pronto, de las botellas de aguardiente, dijo con voz muy baja: «¡Viva París!», como diciendo: «Aquí no nos importan las facultades, ni la técnica, ni la maestría. Nos importa otra cosa.»

Entonces *La Niña de los Peines* se levantó como una loca, tronchada igual que una llorona medieval, y se bebió de un trago un gran vaso de cazalla como fuego, y se sentó a cantar sin voz, sin aliento, sin matices, con la garganta abrasada, pero... con duende. Había logrado matar todo el andamiaje de la canción para dejar paso a un duende furioso y abrasador, amigo de los vientos cargados de arena, que hacía que los oyentes se rasgaran los trajes casi con el mismo ritmo con que se los rompen los negros antillanos del rito lucumí, apelotonados ante la imagen de Santa Bárbara.

On one occasion, the Andalusian flamenco singer Pastora Pavón, *La Niña de los Peines* (The Girl with the Combs), a sombre Hispanic genius with an imagination matching that of Goya or Rafael *El Gallo*,* was singing in a small tavern at Cádiz. She sang with her voice of shadow, with her voice of liquid metal, with her moss-covered voice, and with her voice entangled in her long hair. She would soak her voice in *manzanilla*, or lose it in dark and distant thickets. Yet she failed completely; it was all to no purpose. The audience remained silent.

Among the audience was Ignacio Espeleta, handsome as a Roman tortoise, who was once asked: 'How is it that you never work?', and with a smile worthy of Argantonio, he replied: 'Why should I work if I come from Cádiz?'

Also present was Eloísa, the fiery aristocratic whore of Seville, direct descendant of Soledad Vargas, who in the year 1930 refused to marry a Rothschild because he was not her equal in blood. There were also the Floridas, believed by many to be butchers, while in reality they are ancient priests still sacrificing bulls to Geryon; and in a corner sat that imposing breeder of bulls Don Pablo Murube, looking like a Cretan mask. Pastora Pavón finished singing in the midst of silence. Only a little man, one of those emasculated dancers who suddenly spring up from behind bottles of white brandy, said sarcastically in a very low voice: 'Viva Paris!', as if to say: 'Here we do not care for ability, technique, or mastery. Here we care for something else.'

At that moment *La Niña de los Peines* got up like a woman possessed, broken as a medieval mourner, drank without pause a large glass of *cazalla*, a fire-water brandy, and sat down to sing without voice, breathless, without subtlety, her throat burning but ... with *duende*. She succeeded in getting rid of the scaffolding of the song, to make way for a furious

---

* A famous bullfighter.

La Niña de los Peines tuvo que desgarrar su voz porque sabía que la estaba oyendo gente exquisita que no pedía formas, sino tuétano de formas, música pura con el cuerpo sucinto para poderse mantener en el aire. Se tuvo que empobrecer de facultades y de seguridades; es decir, tuvo que alejar a su musa y quedarse desamparada, que su duende viniera y se dignara luchar a brazo partido. ¡Y cómo cantó! Su voz ya no jugaba, su voz era un chorro de sangre digna por su dolor y su sinceridad, y se abría como una mano de diez dedos por los pies clavados, pero llenos de borrasca, de un Cristo de Juan de Juni.

La llegada del duende presupone siempre un cambio radical en todas las formas. Sobre planos viejos, da sensaciones de frescura totalmente inéditas, con una calidad de rosa recién creada, de milagro, que llega a producir un entusiasmo casi religioso.

En toda la música árabe, danza, canción o elegía, la llegada del duende es saludada con enérgicos «¡Alá, Alá!», «¡Dios, Dios!», tan cerca del «¡Olé!» de los toros, que quién sabe si será lo mismo; y en todos los cantos del sur de España la aparición del duende es seguida por sinceros gritos de «¡Viva Dios!», profundo, humano, tierno grito de una comunicación con Dios por medio de los cinco sentidos, gracias al duende que agita la voz y el cuerpo de la bailarina; evasión real y poética de este mundo, tan pura como la conseguida por el rarísimo poeta del XVII Pedro Soto de Rojas a través de siete jardines, o la de Juan Clímaco por una temblorosa escala de llanto.

and fiery *duende*, companion of sand-laden winds, that made those who were listening tear their clothes rhythmically, like Caribbean Negroes of the lucumí rite clustered before the image of St Barbara.

La Niña de los Peines had to tear her voice, because she knew that she was being listened to by an *élite* not asking for forms but for the marrow of forms, for music exalted into purest essence. She had to impoverish her skills and aids; that is, she had to drive away her muse and remain alone so that the *duende* might come and join in a hand-to-hand fight. And how she sang! Now she was in earnest, her voice was a jet of blood, admirable because of its pain and its sincerity, and it opened like a ten-fingered hand in the nailed but tempestuous feet of a Christ by Juan de Juni.

The appearance of the *duende* always presupposes a radical change of all forms based on old structures. It gives a sensation of freshness wholly unknown, having the quality of a newly created rose, of miracle, and produces in the end an almost religious enthusiasm.

In all Arabic music, dance, or song, the appearance of the *duende* is greeted with vociferous shouts of 'Alá! Alá!', 'God! God!' which are not far from the *olé* of bullfighting. And in the singing of Southern Spain, the presence of the *duende* is followed by shouts of 'Viva Dios!', a profound, human, and tender cry of communion with God through the five senses, by virtue of the *duende* which stirs the voice and body of the dancer, a real and poetical abstraction from this world, as pure as that obtained through seven gardens by the rare seventeenth-century poet Pedro Soto de Rojas,* or by St John Climacus† on his trembling ladder of lament.

---

* Lorca makes reference here to Soto de Rojas' book *Paraíso cerrado para muchos, jardines abiertos para todos*, evocative of the gardens of Granada.

† St John Climacus, sixth-century ascetic, author of the *Scala Spiritualis* or 'Spiritual Ladder'.

Naturalmente, cuando esa evasión está lograda, todos sienten sus efectos: el iniciado, viendo cómo el estilo vence a una materia pobre, y el ignorante, en el no sé qué de una auténtica emoción. Hace años, en un concurso de baile de Jerez de la Frontera, se llevó el premio una vieja de ochenta años contra hermosas mujeres y muchachos con la cintura de agua, por el solo hecho de levantar los brazos, erguir la cabeza y dar un golpe con el pie sobre el tabladillo; pero en la reunión de musas y de ángeles que había allí, belleza de forma y belleza de sonrisa, tenía que ganar y ganó aquel duende moribundo que arrastraba por el suelo sus alas de cuchillos oxidados.

Todas las artes son capaces de duende, pero donde encuentra más campo, como es natural, es en la música, en la danza y en la poesía hablada, ya que estas necesitan un cuerpo vivo que interprete, porque son formas que nacen y mueren de modo perpetuo y alzan sus contornos sobre un presente exacto.

Muchas veces el duende del músico pasa al duende del intérprete, y otras veces, cuando el músico o el poeta no son tales, el duende del intérprete, y esto es interesante, crea una nueva maravilla que tiene en la apariencia, nada más, la forma primitiva. Tal el caso de la enduendada Eleonora Duse, que buscaba obras fracasadas para hacerlas triunfar, gracias a lo que ella inventaba, o el caso de Paganini, explicado por Goethe, que hacía oír melodías profundas de verdaderas vulgaridades, o el caso de una deliciosa muchacha del Puerto de Santa María, a quien yo le vi cantar y bailar el horroroso cuplé italiano *O Mari!*, con unos ritmos, unos silencios y una intención que hacían de la pacotilla italiana una dura serpiente de oro levantado. Lo que pasaba era que, efectivamente, encontraban alguna cosa nueva que nada tenía que ver con lo anterior, que ponían sangre viva y ciencia sobre cuerpos vacíos de expresión.

It follows that when this abstraction is reached, its effects are felt by everyone; by the initiated, who have seen how style can conquer poor matter, and by the ignorant in an indefinable but authentic emotion. A few years ago, in a dancing contest at Jerez de la Frontera, an old woman of eighty carried off the prize against beautiful women and girls with waists like water merely by raising her arms, throwing back her head, and stamping her foot on the platform; in that gathering of muses and angels, beauties of shape and beauties of smile, the moribund *duende*, dragging her wings of rusty knives along the ground, was bound to win and did in fact win.

All the Arts are capable of possessing *duende*, but naturally the field is widest in music, in dance, and in spoken poetry, because they require a living body as interpreter – they are forms that arise and die ceaselessly, and are defined by an exact present.

Often the composer's *duende* passes to the interpreter. It is also worth noting that even if the composer or poet is false, the interpreter's *duende* can create a new marvel bearing little resemblance to the original work. Such was the case of the *duende*-possessed Eleonora Duse, who unearthed failures in order to turn them into successes, by virtue of what she put into them; or of Paganini, who, according to Goethe, could produce profound melodies out of quite commonplace music; or of a delightful girl in Puerto de Santa María whom I once saw sing and dance that frightful Italian song *O Marí!*, with such rhythm, such pauses, and such meaning that she transformed the cheap Italian song into a firm snake of solid gold. In every instance it was indeed a case of the interpreter re-creating the original work: living blood and artistic genius were put into bodies void of expression.

All the Arts, and all countries too, are capable of *duende*, angel, or muse. While Germany has, with some exceptions,

Todas las artes, y aun los países, tienen capacidad de duende, de ángel y de musa; y así como Alemania tiene, con excepciones, musa, y la Italia tiene permanentemente ángel, España está en todos tiempos movida por el duende. Como país de música y danza milenaria, donde el duende exprime limones de madrugada y como país de muerte. Como país abierto a la muerte.

En todos los países la muerte es un fin. Llega y se corren las cortinas. En España, no. En España se levantan. Muchas gentes viven allí entre muros hasta el día en que mueren y los sacan al sol. Un muerto en España está más vivo como muerto que en ningún sitio del mundo: hiere su perfil como el filo de una navaja barbera. El chiste sobre la muerte o su contemplación silenciosa son familiares a los españoles. Desde *El sueño de las calaveras*, de Quevedo, hasta el *Obispo podrido*, de Valdés Leal, y desde la Marbella del siglo XVII, muerta de parto en mitad del camino, que dice:

> *La sangre de mis entrañas*
> *cubriendo el caballo está.*
> *Las patas de tu caballo*
> *echan fuego de alquitrán . . .*

al reciente mozo de Salamanca, muerto por el toro, que clama:

> *Amigos, que yo me muero;*
> *amigos, yo estoy muy malo.*
> *Tres pañuelos tengo dentro*
> *y este que meto son cuatro . . .*

hay una barandilla de flores de salitre, donde se asoma un pueblo de contempladores de la muerte, con versículos de Jeremías por el lado más áspero, o con ciprés fragante por el lado más lírico; pero un país donde lo más importante de todo tiene un último valor metálico de muerte.

a muse, and Italy has permanently an angel, Spain is always moved by the *duende*, being a country of ancient music and dance, where the *duende* squeezes lemons of daybreak, as well as being a nation of death, a nation open to death.

In every country death has finality. It arrives and the curtains are drawn. Not in Spain. In Spain they are lifted. Many Spaniards live between walls until the day they die, when they are taken out to the sun. A dead person in Spain is more alive when dead than is the case anywhere else — his profile cuts like the edge of a barber's razor. The jest about death and the silent contemplation of it is familiar to Spaniards. From Quevedo's 'Dream of the skulls' to the 'Putrescent bishop' of Valdés Leal, and from the Marbella of the seventeenth century, who died in childbirth on the highway, saying:

> *La sangre de mis entrañas*
> *cubriendo el caballo está.*
> *Las patas de tu caballo*
> *echan fuego de alquitrán . . .* ★

to the recent youth of Salamanca, killed by a bull, who exclaimed:

> *Amigos, que yo me muero;*
> *amigos, yo estoy muy malo.*
> *Tres pañuelos tengo dentro*
> *y este que meto son cuatro . . .* †

there is a fence of saltpetre flowers, over which rises a people contemplating death, a people who at their most austere are inspired by the verses of Jeremiah, or at their most lyrical by fragrant cypresses. But also a country where what matters most has the ultimate metallic quality of death.

★ The blood from my womb now covers the horse. The hooves of your horse spark tarry fire . . .

† Friends, I am dying; friends, I am in a bad way. Three handkerchiefs I have inside, and now this is the fourth . . .

La casulla y la rueda del carro, y la navaja y las barbas pinchosas de los pastores, y la luna pelada, y la mosca, y las alacenas húmedas, y los derribos, y los santos cubiertos de encaje, y la cal, y la línea hiriente de aleros y miradores tienen en España diminutas hierbas de muerte, alusiones y voces perceptibles para un espíritu alerta, que nos llenan la memoria con el aire yerto de nuestro propio tránsito. No es casualidad todo el arte español ligado con nuestra tierra, llena de cardos y piedras definitivas, no es un ejemplo aislado la lamentación de Pleberio o las danzas del maestro Josef María de Valdivielso, no es un azar el que de toda la balada europea se destaque esta amada española:

> — *Si tú eres mi linda amiga,*
> *¿cómo no me miras, di?*
> — *Ojos con que te miraba*
> *a la sombra se los di.*
> — *Si tú eres mi linda amiga,*
> *¿cómo no me besas, di?*
> — *Labios con que te besaba*
> *a la tierra se los di.*
> — *Si tú eres mi linda amiga,*
> *¿cómo no me abrazas, di?*
> — *Brazos con que te abrazaba,*
> *de gusanos los cubrí.*

Ni es extraño que en los albores de nuestra lírica suene esta canción:

> *Dentro del vergel*
> *moriré,*

The knife and the cart-wheel, the razor and the prickly beards of shepherds, the bare moon, the fly, damp cupboards, rubble, religious images covered with lacework, quick-lime, and the wounding outline of eaves and watch-towers, in Spain all these have minute grass-blades of death, as well as allusions and voices perceptible to the alert mind, exciting our memory with the inert air of our own passing. The link of Spanish art with the soil is not entirely fortuitous, it is an art abounding in thistles and tangible stones; the lamentation of Pleberio or the dances of the master Josef María de Valdivielso are not isolated examples; it is no accident that from all European balladry this Spanish love-song stands out:

> — *Si tú eres mi linda amiga,*
> *¿cómo no me miras, di?*
> — *Ojos con que te miraba*
> *a la sombra se los di.*
> — *Si tú eres mí linda amiga,*
> *¿cómo no me besas, di?*
> — *Labios con que te besaba*
> *a la tierra se los di.*
> — *Si tú eres mi linda amiga,*
> *¿cómo no me abrazas, di?*
> — *Brazos con que te abrazaba,*
> *de gusanos los cubrí.*★

Neither is it unexpected to find this song among the earliest Spanish lyric poetry:

> *Dentro del vergel*
> *moriré,*

★ 'If you are my sweetheart, why won't you look at me, pray?'
  'Eyes I had to look at thee, to the shadow I gave them.'
  'If you are my sweetheart, why won't you kiss me, pray?'
  'Lips I had to kiss thee, to the earth I gave them.'
  'If you are my sweetheart, why won't you embrace me, pray?'
  'Arms I had to embrace thee, with worms I covered them.'

> dentro del rosal
> matar me han.
> Yo me iba, mi madre,
> las rosas coger,
> hallara la muerte
> dentro del vergel.
> Yo me iba, mi madre,
> las rosas cortar,
> hallara la muerte
> dentro del rosal.
> Dentro del vergel
> moriré,
> dentro del rosal
> matar me han.

Las cabezas heladas por la luna que pintó Zurbarán, el amarillo manteca con el amarillo relámpago del Greco, el relato del padre Sigüenza, la obra íntegra de Goya, el ábside de la iglesia de El Escorial, toda la escultura policromada, la cripta de la casa ducal de Osuna, la Muerte con la guitarra de la capilla de los Benavente en Medina de Rioseco, equivalen en lo culto a las romerías de San Andrés de Teixido, donde los muertos llevan sitio en la procesión, a los cantos de difuntos que cantan las mujeres de Asturias con faroles llenos de llamas en la noche de noviembre, al canto y danza de la Sibila en las catedrales de Mallorca y Toledo, al oscuro *In Record* tortosino y a los innumerables ritos del Viernes Santo, que con la cultísima fiesta de los toros forman el triunfo popular de la muerte española. En el mundo, solamente México puede cogerse de la mano con mi país.

dentro del rosal
matar me han.
Yo me iba, mi madre,
las rosas coger,
hallara la muerte
dentro del vergel.
Yo me iba, mi madre,
las rosas cortar,
hallara la muerte
dentro del rosal.
Dentro del vergel
moriré,
dentro del rosal
matar me han. ★

The moon-frozen heads which Zurbarán painted, the butter-yellow and the lightning yellow of El Greco, the prose of Fr Sigüenza, the whole of Goya's work, the apse of the church at El Escorial, all our polychrome sculpture, the crypt of the ducal house of Osuna, 'Death with the guitar' in the chapel of the Benaventes at Medina de Rioseco, all these are the cultured counterpart of the pilgrimages to St Andrés de Teixido, where the dead have a place in the procession; of the dirges sung by the women of Asturias by lantern-light on the November night; of the dance of the Sibyl in the cathedrals of Majorca and Toledo; of the obscure *In record* from Tortosa; and of the innumerable Good Friday ceremonies which, together with the most civilized spectacle of bullfighting, constitute the popular triumph of death in Spain. Of all the countries in the world, only Mexico can match Spain in this.

★ In the garden I shall die, in the rose-bush I shall be killed. I was going, dear mother, to pick some roses, I found death in the garden. I was going, dear mother, to cut some roses, I found death in the rose-bush. In the garden I shall die, in the rose-bush I shall be killed.

Cuando la musa ve llegar a la muerte cierra la puerta o levanta un plinto o pasea una urna y escribe un epitafio con mano de cera, pero en seguida vuelve a regar su laurel con un silencio que vacila entre dos brisas. Bajo el arco truncado de la oda, ella junta con sentido fúnebre las flores exactas que pintaron los italianos del xv y llama al seguro gallo de Lucrecio para que espante sombras imprevistas.

Cuando ve llegar a la muerte, el ángel vuela en círculos lentos y teje con lágrimas de hielo y narcisos la elegía que hemos visto temblar en las manos de Keats, y en las de Villasandino, y en las de Herrera, y en las de Bécquer y en las de Juan Ramón Jiménez. Pero ¡qué terror el del ángel si siente una araña, por diminuta que sea, sobre su tierno pie rosado!

En cambio, el duende no llega si no ve posibilidad de muerte, si no sabe que ha de rondar su casa, si no tiene seguridad de que ha de mecer esas ramas que todos llevamos y que no tienen, que no tendrán consuelo.

Con idea, con sonido o con gesto, el duende gusta de los bordes del pozo en franca lucha con el creador. Angel y musa se escapan con violín o compás, y el duende hiere, y en la curación de esta herida, que no se cierra nunca, está lo insólito, lo inventado de la obra de un hombre.

La virtud mágica del poema consiste en estar siempre enduendado para bautizar con agua oscura a todos los que lo miran, porque con duende es más fácil amar, comprender, y *es seguro* ser amado, ser comprendido, y esta lucha por la expresión y por la comunicación de la expresión adquiere a veces, en poesía, caracteres mortales.

Recordad el caso de la flamenquísima y enduendada Santa Teresa, flamenca no por atar un toro furioso y darle tres pases magníficos, que lo hizo; ni por presumir de guapa delante de fray Juan de la Miseria ni por darle una bofetada al Nuncio de Su Santidad, sino por ser una de las pocas

As soon as the muse is aware of death, she shuts her door, or raises a plinth, or parades an urn, or writes an epitaph with waxen hand. And she immediately tears her wreath in a silence that wavers between two breezes. Beneath the truncated arch of the ode, she binds with a mournful touch the precise flowers that the Italians painted in the fifteenth century, and summons the dependable cockerel of Lucretius to frighten away unsuspected shadows.

When the angel is aware of death, he slowly circles round, and weaves with icy tears and narcissi the elegy we have seen trembling in the hands of Keats, or Villasandino, or Herrera, or Bécquer, or Juan Ramón Jiménez. But, what a flutter if the angel feels a spider, however minute, on his tender rosy feet!

The *duende*, on the other hand, does not appear if it sees no possibility of death, if it does not know that it will haunt death's house, if it is not certain that it can move those branches we all carry, which neither enjoy nor ever will enjoy any solace.

In idea, in sound, or in gesture, the *duende* likes a straight fight with the creator on the edge of the well. While angel and muse are content with violin or measured rhythm, the *duende* wounds, and in the healing of this wound which never closes is the prodigious, the original in the work of man.

The magical quality of a poem consists in its being always possessed by the *duende*, so that whoever beholds it is baptized with dark water. Because with *duende* it is easier to love and to understand, and also one is *certain* to be loved and understood; and this struggle for expression and for the communication of expression reaches at times, in poetry, the character of a fight to the death.

Let us remember the case of the very flamenca- and *duende*-possessed St Theresa, flamenca not for having stopped a fierce bull with three magnificent passes, which she did; not for having boasted of her good looks in front of Fr Juan

criaturas cuyo duende (no cuyo ángel, porque el ángel no ataca nunca) la traspasa con un dardo, queriendo matarla por haberle quitado su último secreto, el puente sutil que une los cinco sentidos con ese centro en carne viva, en nube viva, en mar viva, del Amor libertado del Tiempo.

Valentísima vencedora del duende, y caso contrario al de Felipe de Austria, que, ansiando buscar musa y ángel en la teología, se vio aprisionado por el duende de los ardores fríos en esa obra de El Escorial, donde la geometría limita con el sueño y donde el duende se pone careta de musa para eterno castigo del gran rey.

Hemos dicho que el duende ama el borde de la herida y se acerca a los sitios donde las formas se funden en un anhelo superior a sus expresiones visibles.

En España (como en los pueblos de Oriente, donde la danza es expresión religiosa) tiene el duende un campo sin límites sobre los cuerpos de las bailarinas de Cádiz, elogiadas por Marcial, sobre los pechos de los que cantan, elogiados por Juvenal, y en toda la liturgia de los toros, auténtico drama religioso donde, de la misma manera que en la misa, se adora y se sacrifica a un Dios.

Parece como si todo el duende del mundo clásico se agolpara en esta fiesta perfecta, exponente de la cultura y de la gran sensibilidad de un pueblo que descubre en el hombre sus mejores iras, sus mejores bilis y su mejor llanto. Ni en el baile español ni en los toros se divierte nadie; el duende se encarga de hacer sufrir por medio del drama, sobre formas vivas, y prepara las escaleras para una evasión de la realidad que circunda.

El duende opera sobre el cuerpo de la bailarina como el aire sobre la arena. Convierte con mágico poder una muchacha en paralítica de la luna, o llena de rubores adolescentes a un viejo roto que pide limosna por las tiendas de vino, da con una cabellera olor de puerto nocturno, y en

de la Miseria, nor for having slapped the Papal Nuncio, but for being one of the few creatures whose *duende* (not whose angel, for the angel never attacks) transfixed her with a dart, wishing her dead for having stolen its last secret – the delicate bridge uniting the five senses with that core made living flesh, living cloud, living sea, of Love freed from Time.

She was a brave vanquisher of the *duende*, in contrast with Philip of Austria, who, hankering after the muse and the angel of Theology, found himself imprisoned by the *duende* of bleak fervours in that edifice of El Escorial, where geometry borders on dream, and where the *duende* wears a muse's mask for the eternal punishment of the great king.

We have said that the *duende* likes the edge of things, the wound, and that it is drawn to where forms fuse themselves in a longing greater than their visible expressions.

In Spain (as in the East, where dance is a religious expression) the *duende* has a boundless field in the bodies of the girl dancers of Cádiz, praised by Martial, in the breasts of singers, praised by Juvenal, and in the whole liturgy of bullfighting, a true religious drama where, as in the Mass, there is adoration and a God is sacrificed.

It is as though the whole *duende* of the classical world converged into this perfect spectacle, symbol of the culture and great sensibility of a people who have discovered man's finest anger, his finest melancholy, and his finest grief. Neither in Spanish dancing nor in bullfighting does anybody have any enjoyment; the *duende* takes care to make one suffer through the drama, in living forms, and prepares the steps for an escape from the surrounding reality.

The *duende* works on the body of a dancer like a breeze on the sand. With magic powers it transforms a girl into a paralytic of the moon, or fills with adolescent blushes an old broken man begging round the taverns, or conveys in tresses of long hair the scent of a harbour at night, and at every

todo momento opera sobre los brazos en expresiones que son madres de la danza de todos los tiempos.

Pero imposible repetirse nunca, esto es muy interesante de subrayar. El duende no se repite, como no se repiten las formas del mar en la borrasca.

En los toros adquiere sus acentos más impresionantes, porque tiene que luchar, por un lado, con la muerte, que puede destruirlo, y por otro lado, con la geometría, con la medida, base fundamental de la fiesta.

El toro tiene su órbita; el torero, la suya, y entre órbita y órbita un punto de peligro donde está el vértice del terrible juego.

Se puede tener musa con la muleta y ángel con las banderillas y pasar por buen torero, pero en la faena de capa, con el toro limpio todavía de heridas, y en el momento de matar, se necesita la ayuda del duende para dar en el clavo de la verdad artística.

El torero que asusta al público en la plaza con su temeridad no torea, sino que está en ese plano ridículo, al alcance de cualquier hombre, de *jugarse la vida*; en cambio, el torero mordido por el duende da una lección de música pitagórica y hace olvidar que tira constantemente el corazón sobre los cuernos.

Lagartijo con su duende romano, Joselito con su duende judío, Belmonte con su duende barroco y Cagancho con su duende gitano, enseñan, desde el crepúsculo del anillo, a poetas, pintores y músicos, cuatro grandes caminos de la tradición española.

moment it works the arms into movements which have generated the dances of all times.

But, it is worth emphasizing, the *duende* can never repeat itself, as the shapes of the sea do not repeat themselves in the storm.

It is in bullfighting that the *duende* attains its most impressive character, because, on the one hand, it has to fight with death, which may bring destruction, and on the other, with geometry, the fundamental basic measure of the spectacle.

The bull has its orbit, the bullfighter his, and between orbit and orbit there exists a point of danger where lies the apex of the terrible game.

It is possible to have muse with the *muleta*★ and angel with the *banderillas*,† and be considered a good bullfighter; but in the work with the cape when the bull is still free of wounds, and again at the final killing, the help of the *duende* is required to hit the nail of artistic truth.

The bullfighter scaring the spectators by his temerity is not bullfighting, he is on the absurd plane of one playing with his life, which anyone can do; on the other hand, the bullfighter who is bitten by the *duende* gives a lesson of Pythagorean music, and we forget that he is constantly throwing his heart at the horns.

Lagartijo with his Roman *duende*, Joselito with his Jewish *duende*, Belmonte with his baroque *duende*, and Cagancho with his gipsy *duende*, from the twilight of the bull-ring they show poets, painters, and musicians, the four great pathways of Spanish tradition.

★ *Muleta*: scarlet cloth folded and doubled over a tapered wooden stick with a sharp steel point.

† *Banderillas*: thin stick with harpoon-like steel point, adorned with coloured paper or flags, and placed in pairs in the withers of the bull to provoke a charge.

España es el único país donde la muerte es el espectáculo nacional, donde la muerte toca largos clarines a la llegada de las primaveras, y su arte está siempre regido por un duende agudo que le ha dado su diferencia y su calidad de invención.

El duende que llena de sangre, por vez primera en la escultura, las mejillas de los santos del maestro Mateo de Compostela, es el mismo que hace gemir a San Juan de la Cruz o quema ninfas desnudas por los sonetos religiosos de Lope.

El duende que levanta la torre de Sahagún o trabaja calientes ladrillos en Calatayud o Teruel es el mismo que rompe las nubes del Greco y echa a rodar a puntapiés alguaciles de Quevedo y quimeras de Goya.

Cuando llueve saca a Velázquez enduendado, en secreto, detrás de sus grises monárquicos; cuando nieva hace salir a Herrera desnudo para demostrar que el frío no mata; cuando arde, mete en sus llamas a Berruguete y le hace inventar un nuevo espacio para la escultura.

La musa de Góngora y el ángel de Garcilaso han de soltar la guirnalda de laurel cuando pasa el duende de San Juan de la Cruz, cuando

> *el ciervo vulnerado*
> *por el otero asoma.*

La musa de Gonzalo de Berceo y el ángel del Arcipreste de Hita se han de apartar para dejar paso a Jorge Manrique cuando llega herido de muerte a las puertas del castillo de Belmonte. La musa de Gregorio Hernández y el ángel de José de Mora han de alejarse para que cruce el duende que llora lágrimas de sangre de Mena y el duende con cabeza de toro asirio de Martínez Montañés; como la melancólica musa de Cataluña y el ángel mojado de Galicia han de

Spain is the only country where death is a natural spectacle, where death blows long fanfares at the arrival of each spring, and its art is always governed by a shrewd *duende* which has given it its distinctive character and its inventive quality.

The *duende* that for the first time in sculpture fills the cheeks of the master Mateo of Compostela's saints with red blood, is the same that makes St John of the Cross moan, or burns naked nymphs in the religious sonnets of Lope de Vega.

The *duende* that raised the tower of Sahagún or worked warm bricks in Calatayud or Teruel, is the same *duende* that breaks the clouds of El Greco and sends Quevedo's bailiffs rolling with a kick, and kindles Goya's visions.

When it rains, it brings out a *duende*-possessed Velázquez, secretly, behind the greys of his monarchs; in the snow it brings out Herrera* naked to prove that coldness does not kill; when the *duende* burns, it draws Berruguete into its blaze, and makes him discover a new dimension in sculpture.

The muse of Góngora and the angel of Garcilaso have to relinquish the laurel wreath when the *duende* of St John of the Cross appears, when

> *el ciervo vulnerado*
> *por el otero asoma.*†

The muse of Gonzalo de Berceo and the angel of the Archpriest of Hita draw aside to let Jorge Manrique pass when he comes to the gates of Belmonte castle mortally wounded. The muse of Gregorio Hernández and the angel of José de Mora have to withdraw to allow the *duende* to pass, weeping Mena's tears of blood. Similarly, the melancholy muse of Catalonia, and the rain-drenched angel of Galicia, have to look with loving wonder at the *duende* of

---

* Juan de Herrera, architect of El Escorial.
† The wounded deer over the hill appears.

mirar, con amoroso asombro, al duende de Castilla, tan lejos del pan caliente y de la dulcísima vaca que pasta con normas de cielo barrido y tierra seca.

Duende de Quevedo y duende de Cervantes, con verdes anémonas de fósforo el uno, y flores de yeso de Ruidera el otro, coronan el retablo del duende de España.

Cada arte tiene, como es natural, un duende de modo y forma distinta, pero todos unen raíces en un punto de donde manan los sonidos negros de Manuel Torre, materia última y fondo común incontrolable y estremecido de leño, son, tela y vocablo.

Sonidos negros detrás de los cuales están ya en tierna intimidad los volcanes, las hormigas, los céfiros y la gran noche apretándose la cintura con la Vía láctea.

Señoras y señores: He levantado tres arcos y con mano torpe he puesto en ellos a la musa, al ángel y al duende.

La musa permanece quieta; puede tener la túnica de pequeños pliegues o los ojos de vaca que miran en Pompeya a la narizota de cuatro caras con que su gran amigo Picasso la ha pintado. El ángel puede agitar cabellos de Antonello de Mesina, túnica de Lippi y violín de Massolino o de Rousseau.

El duende . . . ¿Dónde está el duende? Por el arco vacío entra un aire mental que sopla con insistencias sobre las cabezas de los muertos, en busca de nuevos paisajes y acentos ignorados; un aire con olor de saliva de niño, de hierba machacada y velo de medusa que anuncia el constante bautizo de las cosas recién creadas.

Castille, so remote from the warm bread and the placid cow grazing outside a compass of wind-swept skies and dry earth.

The *duende* of Quevedo and the *duende* of Cervantes, the one with phosphorescent green anemones, and the other with anemones of plaster of Ruidera, crown the altar-piece of the *duende* in Spain.

It is clear that each art has a *duende* of a different kind and form, but they all join their roots at a point where the 'dark sounds' of Manuel Torre emerge, ultimate matter, uncontrollable and quivering common foundation of wood, of sound, of canvas, and of words.

'Dark sounds' behind which we discover in tender intimacy volcanoes, ants, gentle breezes, and the Milky Way clasping the great night to her waist.

Ladies and gentlemen: I have raised three arches and with clumsy hand I have placed in them the muse, the angel, and the *duende*.

The muse remains quiet; she can assume the closely pleated tunic, or the staring cow's eyes of Pompeii, or the large nose with four faces which her friend Picasso gave her. The angel may stir in the tresses painted by Antonello of Messina, or in Lippi's tunic or in the violin of Masolino and of Rousseau.

The *duende* – where is the *duende*? Through the empty arch comes an air of the mind that blows insistently over the heads of the dead, in search of new landscapes and unsuspected accents; an air smelling of a child's saliva, of pounded grass, and medusal veil announcing the constant baptism of newly created things.

Note on the Text

WE HAVE reproduced the poems from the Penguin edition of 1960, which followed the 1957 edition of Lorca's *Obras completas*, published in Madrid. That is the text that Gili – 'but for one or two exceptions' – worked from. (One of these exceptions was for the lecture, 'Juego y teoria del duende'; its pages in his copy of the 1954 edition are well annotated.)

Christopher Maurer has pointed out that Gili made excellent use of the scholarship available in 1959, but that the last few decades have brought new texts and new information to light. We are most grateful to him for giving this book the benefit of his knowledge in the form of comments and corrections which have in many cases been silently incorporated or which have formed the basis of editorial footnotes. These include a few corrections and a number of modern readings which have been incorporated into the Spanish text of the poems; they are footnoted.

We have followed Gili's practice in omitting Lorca's epigraphs, dates and dedications to poems.

The Spanish text of 'Juego y teoria del duende', which was not included in the Penguin edition, comes from the later edition of *Obras completas* edited by Arturo del Hoyo, Madrid: Aguilar, 1986. (In the 1954 edition which Gili used it was entitled 'Teoria y juego del duende'.) Gili's translation omits four short paragraphs of preamble and there are some variants from the 1954 edition which he used, again noted in the text.

Index of First Lines

A las cinco de la tarde 130
Antonio Torres de Heredia 78
Arbol de sangre moja lamañana 156
¡Ay, qué prado de pena! 129
¡Ay qué trabajo me cuesta 50

Bajo el naranjo lava 46

Cada canción 152
Cantan los niños 27
Cien jinetes enlutados 45
Cisne redondo en el río 122
Con una cuchara 96
Córdoba 49
Cuando sale la luna 52

De Cádiz a Gibraltar 153
¿De dónde vienes, amor, mi niño? 127
Desde mi cuarto 56
Dice la tarde: «¡Tengo sed de sombra!» 37

El campo 41
El jovencillo se olvidaba 55
El mar 34
El niño busca su voz 54
El río Guadalquivir 40
Empieza el llanto 42
En la luna negra 48
En la mitad del barranco 63
En un cortijo de Córdoba 58
Equivocar el camino 116
Era hermoso jinete 124
Era mi voz antigua 104
Esquilones de plata 30

He cerrado mi balcón 147

La aurora de Nueva York tiene 103
La luna gira en el cielo 92
La luna vino a la fragua 61

La muerte   47
La niña de bello rostro   51
La piedra es una frente donde los sueños gimen   137
La rosa   150
Las piquetas de los gallos   73
Leñador   57
Los caballos negros son   86

Me he perdido muchas veces por el mar   145
Mi corazón reposa junto a la fuente fría   36
¡Mi soledad sin descanso!   83

Nana, niño, nana   118
Norma de seno y cadera   155
No te conoce el toro ni la higuera   140

Por el East River y el Bronx   109
Por las arboledas del Tamarit   148
Por las orillas del río   53
Por las ramas del laurel   151
¿Por qué duermes solo, pastor?   128

¡Que no quiero verla!   133
Quiero bajar al pozo   146
Quiero dormir el sueño de las manzanas   143

Silencio de cal y mirto   69
Si muero   54
Sobre el monte pelado   43
Sólo tu corazón caliente   58

Un bello niño de junco   75

Verde que te quiero verde   65
Verte desnuda es recordar la Tierra   149
Virgen con miriñaque   44
Voces de muerte sonaron   81

Yo no podré quejarme   107
Yo quiero que el agua se quede sin cauce   142
Y que yo me la llevé al río   71

Index of Titles

Adán	156
Alma ausente	140
¡Ay, qué prado de pena! . . .	129
Balada de la placeta	27
Balada de un día de Julio	30
Balada del agua del mar, La	34
Baladilla de los tres ríos	40
Bodas de sangre	118
Cada canción	152
Camino	45
Canción	51
Canción de jinete	49
Canción de jinete (1860)	48
Canción del naranjo seco	57
Canto nocturno a los marineros andaluces	153
Cantos nuevos	37
Casida de la mujer tendida	149
Casida de la rosa	150
Casida de las palomas oscuras	151
Casida del herido por el agua	146
Casida del llanto	147
Casida de los ramos	148
Cielo vivo	107
Cuerpo presente	137
¿De dónde vienes, amor, mi niño? . . .	127
Deseo	38
Despedida	54
El niño mudo	54
El rey de Harlem	96
Era hermoso jinete . . .	124
Es verdad	50
Gacela de Ia huida	145
Gacela de la muerte oscura	143
Gacela de la terrible presencia	142
Granada y 1850	56

La aurora   103
La casada infiel   71
La cogida y la muerte   130
La guitarra   42
La Lola   46
La luna asoma   52
La monja gitana   69
La sangre derramada   133
Llanto por Ignacio Sánchez Mejías   101

Malagueña   47
Mariana Pineda   58
Monólogo de la luna   122
Muerte de Antoñito el Camborio   81

Nana   118
Norma   155

Oda a Walt Whitman   109

Paisaje   41
Paso   44
Pequeño poema infinito   116
Poema doble del lago Eden   104
¿Por qué duermes solo, pastor? . . .   128
Prendimiento de Antoñito el Camborio   78
Pueblo   43

Reyerta   63
Romance de la Guardia Civil española   86
Romance de la luna, luna   61
Romance de la pena negra   73
Romance de la talabartera   58
Romance del emplazado   83
Romance sonámbulo   65

San Gabriel (Sevilla)   75
Serenata   53
Sueño   36
Suicidio   55

Thamar y Amnón   92

Yerma   127